Understanding Others in a Neurodiverse World

A Radical Perspective on Communication and Shared Meaning

Dr Gemma Williams

Understanding Others in a Neurodiverse World

© Pavilion Publishing & Media

The author has asserted her rights in accordance with the Copyright, Designs and Patents Act (1988) to be identified as the author of this work.

Published by:

Pavilion Publishing and Media Ltd
Blue Sky Offices
25 Cecil Pashley Way
Shoreham by Sea
West Sussex
BN43 5FF

Tel: +44 (0)1273 434 943
Email: info@pavpub.com
Web: www.pavpub.com

Published 2024

All rights reserved. No part of this publication may be reproduced, stored in a retrieval system, or transmitted in any form or by any means, electronic, mechanical, photocopying, recording or otherwise, without prior permission in writing of the publisher and the copyright owners.

A catalogue record for this book is available from the British Library.

ISBN: 978-1-803883-70-0

Pavilion Publishing and Media is a leading publisher of books, training materials and digital content in mental health, social care and allied fields. Pavilion and its imprints offer must-have knowledge and innovative learning solutions underpinned by sound research and professional values.

Authors: Dr Gemma Williams
Editor: Mike Benge
Cover design: Phil Morash, Pavilion Publishing and Media Ltd
Page layout and typesetting: Phil Morash, Pavilion Publishing and Media Ltd
Printing: Independent Publishers Group (IPG)

About the author

Dr Gemma Williams is an autistic autism researcher, musician and ex-beekeeper, living in Sussex. She currently works as a Research Officer on the Wellcome Trust-funded 'Autism: from menstruation to menopause' project, for Swansea University. Gemma is a linguist by heart, but following her ESRC Postdoctoral Fellowship at the University of Brighton in Social Policy, her research interests have extended to more social justice-related issues, including: autistic people's experiences of loneliness, barriers to healthcare for neurodivergent people, sensory environments of public spaces and, most recently autistic reproductive and gynecological healthcare.

Gemma is a member of the Westminster Commission on Autism and an Associate with the National Development Team for Inclusion where she's contributed to a number of commissioned reports, projects and inquiries aimed at improving service provision for autistic and neurodivergent people within the UK, NHS England and Local Authorities.

Acknowledgements

Thank you to all my loved ones who have encouraged me and cheered me along in writing this. Special thanks to Neil Costello for keeping me in allotment veg and laughter during my PhD, to Michelle for always helping me find my feet and to Lewis for your compassion during my final labour.

This book wouldn't be here without Tim Wharton's supervision during my PhD. Thank you – in particular for modelling how to write. Thanks, too, to Elly Ifantidou and Caroline Jagoe and to my examiners Damian Milton and Deidre Wilson. To Angie Hart and the team at the Centre of Resilience for Social Justice: thank you for setting such a wonderful example of collegiality and coproduction in research and for making me feel so at home.

My thanks to the Economic and Social Research Council (ESRC) and the South Coast Doctoral Training Partnership for their grant (number ES/W005697/1) which, among other things, supported my time to develop the proposal for this book.

My thanks to the bees and to the Sussex Ouse.

In loving memory of Annabelle Delicata and dedicated to All Of Us.

Contents

About the author iii

Acknowledgements v

Introduction 1

Section 1
Finding meaning (in a big, big world) 7

Chapter 1: Knowing and understanding by being in the world 9

Chapter 2: Knowing and understanding others 15

Chapter 3: Making sense in a complex world 29

Section 2
Autistic Meaning (and what do we mean by 'autism'?) 45

Chapter 4: So, what is autism? 47

Chapter 5: Autistic language use: a short history 63

Section 3
It takes two: Sharing meaning with an 'Other' 85

Chapter 6: The double empathy problem 87

Chapter 7: Mind the gap 101

Chapter 8: But how's that relevant? 117

Section 4
Divergent minds and diverse societies 131

Chapter 9: The importance of getting it right 133

Chapter 10: The importance of intersectional thinking 147

Chapter 11: Towards a connected, inclusive society 163

Appendix 1:
List of resources from non-speaking and semi-speaking autistic advocates 175

Appendix 2 179

References 181

Introduction

What's this all about, then?

This is a book that is, essentially, about magic.

Human communication really is a kind of magic as far as I can tell. Remember the ping-pong ball-under-a-paper-cup trick from your childhood? The magician has two paper cups placed mouth-down on their star-and-moon-bedazzled tablecloth. Under one cup is a ping-pong ball. The magician tilts the lip of the cup that faces the audience upwards a little so we can see – yes, there is the ping-pong ball in all its glory. The lip of the other cup is tilted and we see that, no, there is no ping-pong ball under the other. Perhaps the magician even lifts the cup right up off the cloth and shows us its hollow inside. Either way: no ping-pong ball. Then comes the magic wand. *Tap, tap, tap, abracadabra!* In front of your very eyes, the ball has jumped invisibly, inexplicably, and now sits proudly under the previously empty cup[1].

Human communication is, you could argue, more or less the same. You start with one person, with one idea. The idea lives in the first person's mind, contained neatly within their body (we often like to think of ideas as residing within brains, but brains really are part of the body). Some magic words are uttered – *abracadabra, blah blah blah* (spoiler: it doesn't matter what the words are) – and invisibly, inexplicably, the idea has jumped inside another person's mind. Words (and verbal communication) are so commonplace and so much part of almost everything we do it's easy to take the way they work for granted. But, as we'll see later in this book, the closer you look at how verbal communication works, the far weirder and far less simple it seems.

So while, at its core, this book is about magic, it's also (according to its title) more specifically about understanding others in a neurodiverse world and the breakdowns in understanding that can occur between autistic and non-autistic people: often referred to as *the double empathy problem* (see Chapter 6).

---

1 But is it the same ball?

The reason for the word 'others' in the title was two-fold. First, it (obliquely) references the *problem of other minds* (more on this in Chapter 2) – a long-standing philosophical question about how we can ever really know anything, with any certainty, about the minds of anyone other than ourselves. This feels like an important question to underscore an exploration of how cross-neurotype mutual understanding is or isn't achieved. Second, it points to the way in which autistic people have historically been, and often continue to be, 'othered' – a phenomenon in which specific individuals or groups are cast outside of what it means to belong to a larger social group. Autistic people experience dehumanisation on systemic and personal levels and it's time to look to how we can bridge the differences experienced by those of dissimilar neurotypes so that we can better understand and accept one another.

Author positionality

It's fair, I think, to give you some information about me before we embark on this journey together, so you can have a better idea of whether I'm someone you'd like as your guide.

Firstly, I'm autistic (*nothing about us without us*). Always have been and always will be, but I didn't receive a diagnosis until my early 30s. I staggered through my teens and 20s from crisis to crisis until I was finally given the missing piece of information[2] that helped me understand why things hadn't been working for me and how to make them work better.

I've always loved languages: I think the early fascination came from observing the musicality of word patterns and sounds, but also from noticing early on how fraught communication can be. I spent a lot of time as a child and young person both feeling misunderstood by, and not always understanding, others. After receiving NASA's (albeit very kind and pamphlet-packed) rejection letter at age 11 and realising exiting the Earth to explore space likely wasn't for me, becoming a linguist seemed the most obvious next choice.

It took a while (nearly 20 years) for me to get there, but having spent some time teaching English as a foreign language, I eventually began a linguistics PhD and some of the work included in this book. I've remained in academia – if you find the right team it can be quite a

---

2 Carefully dodging the cursed 'puzzle-piece' metaphor here!

rewarding and safe little nook – but I've since migrated a little away from pure linguistics towards research anchored more in social justice and health and social care policy. There's some of that in this book too – particularly in the final section.

One final important thing to state early on is that I'm a white autistic person. As you'll discover throughout the book, social context is a really important factor in how well communication works. All the big and small things about who we are, where we've come from and what we look like make a difference to how people interpret what we say. Black and Brown people face systemic racism and prejudice in all walks of life and this undoubtedly affects how their communication is perceived and engaged with. For those who are Black or Brown and autistic, there will be additional layers to the kind of communication breakdowns this book is looking at that I have never experienced. Moreover, if we're honest, the autism research field has a race problem, with Black and Brown autistic people significantly under-represented in research both as participants and as researchers. This means that the data we have available about how communication does and doesn't work well between autistic and non-autistic people is potentially skewed, and certainly doesn't equally represent everyone's experience. In many ways, I'm just one more white person having an opinion about things. My hope, though, is that this book will be useful for *all* autistic people using spoken language to communicate.

Just one final thing about me that might be useful to know: I'm a recovering beekeeper...

What's to come

The flow of this book moves from an introduction to key concepts in cognitive linguistics about meaning and communication, through a potted history of autism, to the main offering: a theory of cross-neurotype communication. The first half of the book (sections 1 and 2) introduces key concepts, and the second half (sections 3 and 4) brings them together before looking at how this might be applied in everyday contexts.

Section 1 – Finding meaning (in a big, big world) – offers an overview of the problem of how we draw meaning from the world. It begins with questions about how living beings experience themselves and others in the world (Chapter 1). We'll look at some different perspectives on how communication and shared meaning is achieved (Chapter 2) and finish (in Chapter 3) with a walk-through of the role of intention recognition in communication and an introduction to a theory that's central to this book: 'relevance theory'.

Section 2 – Autistic meaning (and what do we mean by 'autism'?) – provides a critical summary of what has been meant by the term 'autism' since its conception (Chapter 4), covering the origins of the diagnosis through to more contemporary perspectives, touching on the differences between the medical and social models of disability. Chapter 5 then offers a summary of how autistic language use has been assessed and described from these two opposing paradigms.

In Section 3 – It takes two: sharing meaning with an 'Other' – we come to the central contribution of this book: a suggestion for how we might understand (in cognitive linguistic terms) why communication often breaks down between autistic and non-autistic people. Chapter 6 introduces the double empathy problem in detail, and Chapter 7 shares some parallel theories about how mutual understanding is and isn't achieved between those with diverse dispositions or similar minds. In Chapter 8, all the threads from the previous chapters are woven together and we explore how an enactive, embodied perspective of autistic communicators can work with relevance theory to account for the double empathy problem.

Lastly, in Section 4 – Divergent minds and diverse societies – we'll consider what this all means in the context of diverse societies. Chapter 9 first looks at the social exclusion of autistic people and the concept of *ethical loneliness*. Chapter 10 thinks intersectionally about how co-existing dimensions of 'difference' add to the communication breakdowns that autistic people often experience and how that impacts access to services and quality of life. Finally, Chapter 11 looks towards an inclusive society and summarises some key communication recommendations in the contexts of health, social care and education.

Final word

This is a book that explores a cognitive linguistic interpretation of breakdowns in spoken communication between autistic and non-autistic people. As such, its primary focus is communication involving *autistic people who use speech and words to communicate most (if not all) of the time*. There are a large number of autistic people who are non-speaking, some or all of the time, and this book does not really cover those experiences. That's not because their experience is not important: quite the opposite. The theories explored here work best for explaining spoken, verbal communication[3] and although I think they *might* still work in the context of Augmentative and Alternative Communication (AAC), there are probably more useful theories and certainly more knowledgeable people with lived experience who have more important things to say about it (*nothing about us without us*). At the back of the book there is a list of resources, social media accounts, and suggested reading to hear directly from non-speaking autistic people (see Appendix 1).

At the start of this introduction, I promised magic, and I'm aware that is a high expectation to set. But as American philosopher and cultural ecologist David Abram (1996: 9) has said, magic, ultimately, is the 'experience of existing in a world made up of multiple intelligences'. What greater act of transformational magic could there be than understanding other minds (in a neurodiverse world…)?

Thank you so much for reading. Let's go!

---

3   Although non-verbal communication features – things like gesture and intonation – definitely play a part in these discussions.

Section 1
Finding meaning (in a big, big world)

Chapter 1: Knowing and understanding by being in the world

Being in the world

For almost the entirety of my PhD, I lived on a boat.

I'd sit out on the back deck in my rocking chair of a still evening, wrapped in a coarse, woollen blanket with a mug of black coffee balanced on the worn, rusty step of the ladder. When the tide was out, I'd let my eyes rest on the silty mudflats around me, black-headed gulls performing slapstick for each other in the shallows, chasing out ribbon-worms to the sound of tiny passerines – bluetits and sparrows – wittering behind me as they chanced the short stretch from gnarled buddleia to the feeder I'd left swinging from the bow's awning. If the river was up, I'd watch cormorants curl their long, oil-coloured dinosaur necks below the river's meniscus, piercing the fast-blooming reflections of the burnt-out warehouse-husk on the opposite shoreline, or watch the water broil with upstreaming mullet. This was where I did most of my thinking, and where, for a long time, I felt most at one with the world.

Feeling at one with the world is a strange expression. It gives the impression that our connectedness with the world around us is only ever a fleeting thing: just a feeling. And while, it's true, our sense of belonging to and with those around us and to the natural world does come and go, we never actually stop being in the world. We *are* the world. We're all made of the same matter. And, when you zoom in close enough, the distinction between *what's me* and *what's not me* becomes blurrier and blurrier. My physical body, for example, hums along in consort with myriad mutualistic micro-organisms who, among other functions, help me digest and utilise the mass of plant bodies I consume to keep myself alive and well. The *me* bit of 'me' that feels like it's having these thoughts and directing my fingers to type them, despite having an identifiable consistency across my lifetime, has absolutely been shaped and altered by my interactions with others and the world around me.

But what do cormorants and micro-organisms have to do with cross-neurotype communication, you may well be wondering? Well, while this is a book interested specifically in communication between autistic and non-autistic speakers – and, I promise, we will get to that – at its core this is a book about how we can achieve mutual understanding with those who are different to ourselves. How can we peaceably co-exist with those with different *ways of being*?[4] Perhaps, now more so than ever, that is a skill all of us could benefit from developing.

Before we can go much further, we first need to cover some key concepts about ourselves as cognising agents in the world, with minds that work hard to make sense of the worlds around us. This first chapter, then, is a short skip and a hop through of some of these foundational ideas before we move on, in Chapter 2, to looking in closer detail at how one mind can come to know and understand another by means of (verbal) communication.

Embodied and enactive minds

> *'The body is that mysterious and multifaceted phenomenon that seems to accompany one's awareness, and indeed to be the very location of one's awareness...'*
>
> Abram (1996 :37)

In the mid-1980s, the cognitive sciences (i.e. those disciplines interested in understanding how the mind and brain work) were dominated by a cognitivist paradigm: one that centred around the metaphor of the mind as a computer. Against this backdrop, an alternative view was beginning to take hold. Rather than brains (as houses of the mind) processing *representations* of the outside world (as perceived by our various sensory organs) the emphasis moved towards minds as being intrinsically *embodied* and socially and materially *embedded* in the world.

The idea of the *embodied mind* holds that cognition (i.e. the ability to know) is really only possible because of the body which, in turn,

---

4 More on divergent *ways of being* in Chapter 4.

is *embedded* within its social and material environments. Historically – certainly as far back as Descartes (1998) – the common notion was that material bodies were nothing more than *beast-machines*, elevated (in the unique case of human animals) by an ephemeral consciousness and reason. The *embodiment* argument moves us beyond this towards a material explanation for thought and cognition: seeing us as thinking, dreaming matter[5]. Even more than that, in the field of consciousness studies, the experience of possessing and regulating a distinct body within the world is now thought of as one of 'the most basic aspects of conscious selfhood upon which higher-level properties of selfhood, such as the experience of being a distinctive individual across time, may rest' (Seth & Tsakiris, 2018: 3). For our purposes, the idea of the mind as embodied is an important one – considering the fact that autistic people often experience divergent sensory and embodied realities – and one that we'll keep revisiting throughout this book.

Enactivism

Enactivism is the third strand of the new turn in cognitive science (and the third 'E' in what is sometimes referred to as '3E cognition' – cognition that is *embodied, embedded and enactive*). What both embodied and enactive theories of cognition share is a phenomenological framing of an individual's external reality as inextricably linked to their experience of it: as filtered through their body. In enactivism, the emphasis is placed on the online relationship between brain, nervous system and external environment, where the environment is understood to be, at least in part, enacted (created) by the intelligent inter-relation of sensorimotor faculties and whatever it is that is actually 'out there'.

Embodied and enactive theories of cognition (see: Clark 1997; 2013; 2015; Varela *et al*, 1991) share the essential belief that mental processes cannot be easily teased apart from the constraints of the body. Enactivism takes this one step further and argues that the (perceived) world is, in part, 'brought forth' (Di Paolo *et al*, 2018) by a cognisor's embodied interactions with it. Brains are seen more as 'controllers for embodied activity' (Clark, 1997: xii) as opposed to fleshy machines computing data acquired via sensory and perceptual receptors. Living and cognising is seen as an integrated activity where action, perception and cognition interweave to

---

5 More on this and how something called 'predictive processing' tries to explain the mechanics of the embodied mind in Chapter 7.

keep precarious, autonomous organisms alive. Living organisms are active participants in their environments, not simply passive recipients of data.

Autopoiesis

The enactive view of cognition is built around the idea of *autopoiesis* (i.e. self-organisation), proposed by biologists Maturana and Varela (1991) to differentiate living organisms from inanimate matter. According to the theorists, any *autopoietic* (i.e. self-maintaining) agent has a biological imperative to resist a natural tendency towards disorder, or *entropy*. In a constantly changing environment, state preservation is essential for survival.

In what will certainly be an imperfect example (as I'm a linguist, not a biologist), if I were to drop a blob of ink into a dish of water, over time we would see it begin to dissipate. An ink blob is inanimate and has no sense of selfhood: thus has no imperative (or ability) to preserve its own integrity. Ultimately, entropy ensues and our intrepid ink-blob-in-water becomes one small part of a larger inky-water. Conversely, as a self-maintaining human organism, if suboptimal levels of hydration are detected within my body, I'll become thirsty: a physiological prompt to drink more water and rehydrate, thus resisting entropy.

The concept of autopoiesis is certainly much more complex than this – focused as it is on micro biochemical and energetic exchanges of an organism with its environment – but for our purposes we really only need to hold on to the sense that embodied, enactive agents such as ourselves exist in calculated harmony with their environments in a way that is thought to bring about and shape both cognition itself and the experienced world we participate in.

Worlds and *Umwelten*

One final term that will be useful throughout this book, also closely related to the idea of enactive cognition is the concept of *Umwelt*. Originally coined by late 20th century German biologist Jacob von Uexküll, *Umwelt* describes the environment as it experienced by any living organism. *Umwelten* (the plural) are those distinct phenomenal worlds in which organisms are perceiving, acting subjects: 'worlds strange to us but known to other creatures, manifold and varied as the animals themselves' (Von Uexküll, 1992: 319).

As an example, imagine, if you can, the Umwelt of the humble honeybee. Her location in three-dimensional space is demarcated by the vectors of herself, the hive entrance and the position of the sun as it moves through the sky in a constantly recalibrating equation. Star and cross shapes leap out of the landscape while compact round shapes fade into the background, directing her flight across the meadow towards opened flowers rather than to shut buds. Ultraviolet landing strip patterns on petals, invisible to humans, direct her to nectar-filled cups at the heart of the flower. Of the multitude of phenomena in the natural world, it is only those that are 'biologically meaningful' (Von Uexküll, 1992: 327) to an organism that will 'shine forth from the dark like beacons' and act as sign stimuli, affecting recognition by its receptor organs (Von Uexküll, 1992: 325). The world we know is precisely just so, because it serves us best to be attuned to it this way.

As we move through this book, we'll revisit each of the above several times – but particularly so in Chapters 7 and 8, when our theory-building crescendos. For now, let's turn our gaze to what happens to when two cognisors interact and attempt to communicate information about the world with one another and look at how, for humans, communication often involves some kind of *mind-reading*.

Chapter 2: Knowing and understanding others

To the northerly tip of the island, beyond the graveyard of dilapidated boats, lay a small plot of unused land. Deciding to take advantage of the grinding-to-a-halt that had occurred with a sudden national 'lockdown' response to the global Covid-19 crisis, the owners of the boatyard where my houseboat was moored launched an enthusiastic clearing of the overgrowth. As the digger compressed discarded bilge pumps and jerry cans into the ground, crushing rusty paint tins and broken masts, out through thick ribbons of bramble and knots of bindweed, emerged my long-abandoned beehive. Within a day, a swarm had discovered it. The hive I'd left to become weed-shrouded and webbed two summers ago, following a devastating wasp invasion that had killed my colony of ten years, was now humming, and alive…

A week later, in the high heat of late May, I returned to find thousands of bees smothering the face of the recently repainted hive. Around the dark entrance slit, I had coloured two red lips: lips that now murmured as the mouth of a bearded lady.

I had, of course, heard of 'bearding' bees before but never, in 15 years, had I experienced it myself. As days and nights passed with the temperature dropping and the throng remaining on the outside, I became increasingly concerned. I thumbed through the antique beekeeping books growing slowly damp on my boat bookshelves. I Googled. Nothing made sense. I sat one evening at dusk before the hive, half-balanced awkwardly on a lump of concrete, and asked the bees, aloud:

'Are you okay? What do you need from me?'

The answer was not forthcoming.

But why should it be? The bees — these particular bees — were not familiar to me, nor I to them. I had not yet learned the colony's character or their ways, and I was 18 months out of the daily practice of being around any bees whatsoever.

As I watched them slide one over another like dark treacle, humming gently and fanning their wings, I felt decidedly out of sync…

Communicating in code

The sensorium (or sensory-perceptual tools) of the European honeybee – *apis mellifera mellifera* – is extraordinarily rich. They're the sommeliers of the plant world and alchemists of sweet aromatic substances. As such, their olfactory (smelling) and gustatory (tasting) senses are predictably acute. So too is their specialised *mechanosensation*: a sense adapted to perceive fine detail through vibration. But above all, it is their vision that inspires most envy. Honeybee vision, just like human vision, is trichromatic (i.e. they see in full colour), but spectrally shifted towards the ultraviolet end at the expense of some of the deeper red shades (Avarguès-Weber *et al*, 2012). With a 'shutter' rate five times that of human sight (Riddle, 2016), bees can rapidly pick out the hues of single flowers within a dense meadow as they fly at speed. In addition to the intricate patterns of ultraviolet fluorescence on petals that guide bees to nectar sources, startling, sporadic flashes of light-plasma erupt from the swinging power cables that criss-cross their paths from hive to pollen source during episodes of (man-made) corona discharge (Tyler *et al*, 2014). As backdrop to all this is the sky, rippled with textured, 'polarised light' that can aid in orientation when the sun and other navigational celestial bodies are occluded by clouds (Kraft *et al*, 2011: 707).

Honeybees travel vast distances in search of sources of nourishment (they will comfortably, and repeatedly, fly as far as three miles for a good pollen flow and then back again) and must be able to communicate the location of the food sources they have discovered to a precise degree of detail in an ever-changing environment. They have evolved to possess what amounts to a highly complex cognitive system, and a unique means of effectively conveying elaborate information, the most famous example of which is the *waggle dance*.

In the very first instance, no dance is performed unless foraging by further bees is worthwhile, i.e. unless there is sufficient pollen or nectar to merit the journey. The very fact that a dance is performed communicates that a calculation has been made and a beneficial effect has been anticipated. The waggle dance is used for those instances when food sources are 100m or further from the hive. The scent attached to the dancer alerts her audience to the type of flower in question, and the exuberance of the waggle indicates the potential magnitude of the haul. The tempo of the movement (a squat figure-of-eight progression) communicates the distance of travel and the direction is described in the orientation of the central line of the eight (see *Figure 1*.)

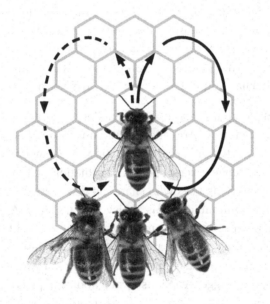

Figure 1: The tail-wagging dance. Three followers are receiving the message (adapted from von Frisch, 1967: 57).

As we saw in Chapter 1, all autopoietic organisms (i.e. things which are alive and motivated to maintain a molecular reaction network contained within a boundary of itself) interact with their environment on the basis of what is 'biologically meaningful' (Von Uexküll, 1992: 327). For example, in the case of honeybees, pollen provides a rich source of amino acids required to nurture growing larvae. That pollen is a vital source of nutrition for bees is not an inherent property of pollen itself. In fact, from a plant perspective, pollen is a mass of the precious gamete-containing micro-spores (in other words, plant sperm). Organisms exist in constant inter-relation with their environment, experiencing the world through, and as, their *Umwelt*. From this perspective, 'living is sense-making' (Thompson, 2004: 386).

Within the framing of such worlds, organised and experienced as they are by salient information necessary to promote the survival of any given organism, possessing the ability to share and to be the recipient of shared information surely confers some advantage. Communication, even in its most rudimentary form, functions as 'a form of belief and desire transfer: cognition by proxy' (Origgi & Sperber, 2000: 150). As the scout bee loops her infinity symbol across the comb, waggling her tail with enthusiasm, complex information is transmitted from one organism to another, in a manner that makes clear sense to the receiver: *A productive source of pollen exists, worth the flight of several bees; 1313m away; 243° WSW*. Communication then, in all forms, can be thought of as an adaptive evolutionary mechanism. But how on earth does it work?

For non-human communication, a code model seems to be a sufficient explanation. Indeed, from Aristotle up until only around 50 years ago, the code model was the preferred explanation. A bee will perform her waggle dance to encode certain specific information that may easily be decoded by observing bees who share the bee-code. All across the animal kingdom, communication is achieved in this way. Arguably, in parts of the plant world, too; in a meta-analysis of many different studies, botanists Karban, Yang and Edwards (2014) found widespread evidence that a diverse range of plants emit volatile compounds following attack by a herbivore, that trigger reactions in neighbouring plants which reduce their own vulnerability to attack. All that is required for this kind of code-based communication to work is that the signifier (a symbol, a sound, a chemical, etc) remains consistently wedded to the signified (the concept it represents). In the case of plants under attack, certain compounds released into the air carry the encoded message to their nearby plant brethren that danger is afoot[6].

---

6   Yes, the plants are essentially screaming...

To an extent, this model also works for human communication. Language may be seen as a repertoire of sounds (phonemic representations) and associated written (orthographic) symbols paired with meanings (see Chapter 3 for more about meaning) that is organised by a natural grammar (syntax) that can potentially create infinite combinations (see Chomsky, 2000). If I'm out rambling on a country path in the UK (where I'm based), it's common practice to greet any passerby. I spot someone scrambling up the slippery chalk path toward me. I (the *source*), *encode* my *message* (a simple greeting) into sounds which I vocalise. The *receiver* (the passerby) receives this *signal* through their auditory *channel* and – if they speak English –*decodes* my noises into the nice polite greeting of 'Hello there!'

The code model kind of works here, and does too for at least a portion of human communication (both linguistic and *paralinguistic*: all the extra gestural and tone of voice 'stuff') but there is much more yet that remains unaccounted for by it. Language has evolved as something wondrously (and necessarily) complex, but as such, it always takes place at a risk. Human meaning has room for slippage in a way that a honeybee's meaning does not. In Chapter 3, we'll look at an alternative model that hopes to take account of that wibbly-wobbliness of words and language – the *inferential model* of communication – but first, let's take a look at something that humans seem to do uniquely in the way they interact with one another and ascribe meaning to another's actions.

Marvellous mind-readers

Remember I said this book was essentially about magic? Humans, it seems, are all *mind-readers*. Somehow, we know what's in the minds of others, often with very few external clues. I'm driving behind you in my car and I can tell, by something about how your car is moving, that you're thinking about taking a right turn coming up soon, even though the turning hasn't yet come into sight. Or you pass me in the supermarket and something about the way I'm striding, swinging my basket lets you know I'm in a terrible mood.[7] Maybe, instead, you walk past the slightly ajar door of a colleague's office at the end of the day and you hear them absent-mindedly singing to themself or letting out a loud belch and you know that they believed they were alone and out of earshot.

---

7   Not very likely as I can rarely face the sensory overwhelm of being in a busy supermarket, but for the purposes of argument...

For a long time now, philosophers, cognitive scientists, neuroscientists and social scientists have all grappled with this feat of magic, often referred to as the *problem of other minds*. They've been troubled by the question: how is it that we seem to know the mental states of others? And, come to think of it, how can we even explain knowing for sure that others are also thinking beings with internal worlds, given that we can only observe the externalised behaviour of others?[8]

The answer may seem intuitive: *of course* we know that others have their own unique thoughts, beliefs, desires, emotions and intentions. But how do we know that? You may think this understanding comes from our ability to tell each other what we're thinking – using language – but as we'll see in the following chapter, we really need to already be able to imagine the thoughts of others in order to be able to understand what they say. Okay then, so maybe it's because you can assume that another person, being a human (like you, I assume, if you're reading this book), will function in a very similar way. You have thoughts and feelings, so everyone else must do, too, right? And somehow this similarity also helps us to 'mind-read' another person's states, perhaps based on behavioural clues? Seems reasonable. But how about that age-old quandary you've possibly found yourself musing over, the one involving our qualia (the name philosophers give to the phenomenal aspects of our mental lives that paint the portrait of what it is like to experience being a 'me' in the world)...

Imagine, you're sitting with a friend watching a beautiful sunset. You both gasp as the sky transmutes dimming blue into a stunning peachy-red and you agree how glorious this colour is, what a wonder nature is. But then it strikes you: how can you know if the colour you're seeing is the exact same colour seen by your companion? There's no definitive way to tell whether your 'peachy-red' is actually closer to your friend's 'pale pink', their 'orange' or even their 'electric blue'. No matter how fine-grained you get with your language in describing what you see, the words don't carry any meaning themselves. They just *represent* a phenomenon in the world (as you understand it from your perspective) and a phenomenon from your friend's perspective: and we hang on the hope that the phenomena are somehow similar enough.[9]

---

8   Philosophers love over-complicating things.
9   Here lies that slippage in meaning that honeybees and their code-based communication don't need to worry about.

In truth, none of us can ever completely understand the unique subjective experience of another. As we saw in Chapter 1, while we all exist in the shared, objective, material world (or *Welt*, in German), we each have our own *Umwelt*: a personalised web of significances, shaping how we perceive and experience it. Our perceptions of the world around us are always framed by our unique perspectives, our cultural backgrounds, and – importantly – our bodies. However, while we may not ever be able to know the world exactly as another person knows it, we can often approximate their perspective and experience to a 'good enough' degree. Enter the magic wand, *theory of mind*.

Theory of mind

Humans are, undoubtedly, highly social animals. Being able to interact with others in social groups has been an important evolutionary function. Accurately predicting how others will act is a skill we've honed over hundreds of thousands of years and our brains apportion a lot of resources to getting this right. Yet this skill – theory of mind – happens so quickly and is so integral to almost everything we do, we rarely notice we're doing it...

According to Premack and Woodruff (1978: 515):

> *'An individual has a theory of mind if he imputes mental states to himself and others. A system of inferences of this kind is properly viewed as a theory, because such states are not directly observable, and the system can be used to make predictions about the behaviour of others.'*

This ability to attribute mental states (such as beliefs, intentions, desires and emotions) to others seems to be particularly human. It shapes our social interactions and scaffolds language abilities. However, there do seem to be a number of non-human animals that also exhibit similar faculties, though to perhaps a lesser degree.

For example, in one seminal study, having watched video recordings of human actors apparently experiencing a range of different problems, chimpanzees seemed to be able to select the appropriate solution to resolve the human's issue (Premack & Woodruff, 1978), thus indicating an ability to *know* the human actors' desires (e.g. trying to escape a locked cage, or trying to reach some high-hanging bananas). In another study, apes demonstrated a sensitivity to human intentions by behaving more sympathetically to individuals who intended to feed them but were unable (Krupenye & Call, 2019). Rhesus macaques and capuchin monkeys have also been seen to be sensitive to others' goals and intentions; corvids (such as ravens, crows and jays) seem to be sensitive to what others can see and hear from their independent perspectives; and dogs (as any dog-guardian will surely attest) seem canny enough to their humans' perspectives to, for example, do 'secret' things when out of sight (e.g. gorging on prohibited snacks or stealing food), which rely on knowing what their humans can and can't see (Krupenye & Call, 2019).

If, as Premack and Woodruff highlight, these mental states (beliefs, desires, intentions, etc.) aren't directly observable, how is it that we are able to accurately infer them in such volumes and at such speed on a moment-to-moment basis? Spoiler alert: despite its significance for human social cognition, the exact mechanisms behind theory of mind and even whether it's one broad cognitive skill or a suite of constituent abilities, remains unclear. There are, however, two strong contender theories: namely the *simulationist* account and the *theory theory*[10] account.

According to the simulationist account of theory of mind, our ability to infer the states of others is rooted in our own experience. Your ability to understand that your friend is sad when they tell you, with a quiver in their voice and their eyes downcast, that their pet axolotl has perished, is founded on recollections of your own comparable losses and your ability to apply this to your friend's present situation. You theorise how your friend must be feeling based on how *you* would feel in the same scenario and how you might be feeling if your own voice were beginning to quiver. A theory-theory account of the same scenario is slightly more rules-based. In order to imagine how your friend is feeling you draw instead on your general world knowledge of how you've learned people typically feel in such a situation, and when displaying such behaviour. You base your interpretation on what you've seen before, what the common tropes are in films or books, what you've been taught in school or by the cultural norms you live by. In both cases – the simulationist and theory-theory accounts of theory mind – you use what you know and apply it to the context at high speed, and voila: you're a mind-reader.

---
10 Yes, really. (I didn't name them...)

Issues with the theory of mind concept

While it has been a useful way of thinking about how we can know what's in another's mind, there are a number of issues with the theory of mind concept itself, and a lot of more recent research has challenged some of the early studies that this theory is based on. This matters because – as we'll see in more detail in Chapter 5 – theory of mind has been described as the 'quintessential ability that makes us human' (Baron-Cohen, 2001: 174), yet traditionally, autistic people have often been described as lacking this ability. Let's, for now, rise above the evident ableism there[11] and review some of the critiques of the theory.

It's all a bit vague

One of the main problems with theory of mind is that it's a little bit unclear what it is, and what's actually involved. It's often taken for granted that (neurotypical) adults will have flawless theory of mind performance, and yet many studies now show that this isn't the case, and that adults often fail to use their theory of mind skills in certain situations (Samson & Apperly, 2010).

Additionally, we now know that theory of mind abilities don't solely rely on the possession of theory of mind concepts, but on a suite of processes that exploit them at speed. In order to properly gauge someone else's perspective, you need to, in the first instance, *have* a theory of mind (i.e., be able to imagine another person's unique perspective that's different from your own). You then need to be able to resist the (strong) influence of your own ego-centric perspective. Next, you'll need to 'select, monitor and integrate the relevant cues' from the current situation, weighing up what facts or individuals might be pertinent, and over what timeframe. Finally, you can use your reasoning skills to combine all of this information and determine the other person's mental state content (Samson & Apperly, 2010: 7). This is absolutely as mental-energy-intensive as it sounds, and surprise-surprise, as adults we often take shortcuts to avoid some of these steps when we want to conserve mental energy.

Ages and stages

A lot of theory of mind research – and particularly the earlier pieces that have shaped how we think about autistic people's theory of mind – has been based on studies almost exclusively involving pre-school-aged

---

[11] Worry not, we'll be revisiting this.

children (i.e. children under the age of 5). In fact, just four percent of over 6,000 published theory-of-mind studies included older children (Hughes, 2016, in Peterson & Wellman, 2018). This is possibly on account of the fact that it is at around that age that neurotypical, hearing children start passing the 'false belief' test. At this age, autistic children tend to have a more mixed performance. However, one more recent study may have identified why that might be. Researchers Peterson and Wellman tested children between the ages of three and 11 over a year and a half with tests that measured six different aspects of theory of mind:

1. 'Diverse desires' (different people can want different things).
2. 'Diverse beliefs' (people can believe different things).
3. 'Knowledge access' (seeing a thing leads to knowing about it and not seeing it leads to ignorance of it).
4. 'False belief' (people can believe things that aren't true).
5. 'Hidden emotion' (people can hide their true feelings behind false expressions).
6. 'Sarcasm' (people can mean the opposite of what they say).

What the researchers found was that despite previous expectations, 'most autistic children, like their typically developing and Deaf peers, do continue to make substantial longitudinal theory of mind progress during the school years' (Peterson & Wellman, 2019: 1931). The autistic children *weren't* demonstrating the same level of theory of mind skills at the same age as neurotypical children, but they *did* demonstrate steady individual progress that had been missed in studies focused on younger children. And perhaps even more significantly, they also found that autistic children developed these theory of mind skills in a different sequence to neurotypical children in their study. In other words, at the stage when neurotypical children are usually acquiring 'false belief' skills, autistic children are instead developing the 'hidden emotions' skill, which usually comes later.[12]

Tools

The various different tools and tests used to measure theory of mind skills and concepts have also come under some criticism. In a review of all the

---

[12] Side note: I can't help but notice how interesting it is that autistic children learn that expressions don't always match feelings earlier that neurotypical children, considering our own expressions are often read as 'wrong' according to neurotypical norms.

various studies to date (2019 at the time of the review) found that many of the original findings (on which the long-standing belief that autistic people lack theory of mind was based) weren't often replicated in subsequent versions of similar tests (Gernsbacher & Yergeau, 2019). They also found that the different tests of theory of mind didn't seem, statistically, to be measuring comparable things.

One of the main research tools used in theory-of-mind research with autistic children – a 'false belief' test known as the 'Sally-Anne task' – has received particular critique in more recent years. 'False belief' tests aim to see whether an individual can hold in mind the idea that someone else can have a belief about something that is false. In the Sally-Anne task, a child is asked to observe a short scene unfold in which one character (Sally) puts an object (some chocolate or a marble) into a basket and then leaves the room. While outside of the room, the second character (Anne) removes and hides the chocolate and the child is then asked where Sally will look for it when she comes back. The idea is the child should be able to know that Sally *doesn't know* the chocolate has been moved because she (Sally) hasn't seen this happen: only the child has. If the child can say that Sally will look in the basket where she left the chocolate (and not in Anne's new hiding place), we know the child is able to represent Sally's perspective as different to their own.

In these early 'false belief' studies autistic children seemed to do more poorly at this test than neurotypical children and this has often been taken as hard evidence that autistic children can't represent the minds of others. But, as some have pointed out, passing the test requires abilities other than theory of mind, and there is more to theory than mind than is tested (Bloom and German, 2000). Moreover, some research (Bagnall *et al*, 2022) has shown that autistic children have a marked difficulty with deceiving (though research remains inconclusive as to whether that's an inability to deceive or an aversion to doing so). It's not impossible that there might be an element at play where the autistic child participants in these early studies were struggling to repress the 'truth' as they know it (where the marble *actually* is) rather than an inability to perspective-take. Finally, in a thought experiment about how our similarity with others affects our ability to understand and empathise (more about this in Chapter 7), some researchers have asked how the results of a 'false belief' task might be affected if Sally (for whatever reason) was thought of as being a suspicious type? Perhaps the child is naturally suspicious and imagines Sally to be the same. In this case, it is plausible that Sally would first check her hunch that Anne has hidden her treasured item, meaning that a child thinking of this character that way might answer that Sally would go straight to where the marble was hidden...

And it is not only the Sally-Anne task which has received criticism. In a new review published at the end of 2023, Higgins and colleagues challenged the construct validity[13] of another well-used measure, the 'Reading the Mind in the Eyes Test' (RMET). The RMET involves participants looking at black-and-white photographs of people's eyes (isolated from the rest of their face in a kind of letter-box-shaped window) and choosing the most appropriate of four suggested adjectives to describe the mental state of the person in the image (e.g. 'aghast', 'terrified', 'baffled' or 'mistrustful'). While the RMET is widely accepted as a gold-standard test for social cognitive ability, and used in high-stakes clinical settings[14], the researchers found that 63% of the studies included in the review (over 1,600 independent studies) failed to provide validity evidence from any of the six categories the researchers were using as measures. The TLDR (too-long-didn't-read) version? Reading the Mind in the Eyes Test scores and the research findings based on them are 'unsubstantiated and uninterpretable' (Higgins *et al*, 2023). Ouch.

Building rapport and tuning in

Rapport is one final dimension of how we relate to and understand one another that deserves some brief attention in this chapter, not least because it shows up as a property that's measured and compared in interactions involving those of similar and different neurotypes later (in Chapter 5). Rapport is a highly intuitive characteristic of interaction. It's the feeling-good-ness about our connection with another person: something about how effortless and fluid an interaction is. In technical terms, rapport is often described using a definition set out by Tickle-Degnen and Rosenthal (1990) as involving *mutual attentiveness* (i.e. creating focused and cohesive interaction), *mutual affective-emotional positivity* (i.e. creating mutual good feeling), and *behavioural coordination* (or, in other words, being 'in sync').

---

13 I.e. how successfully a test measures what it was designed to measure.
14 Including during brain surgery.

This feeling-good-ness in social interaction helps to forge social bonds and build trust. It also helps to build a shared understanding of reality (Gaertner & Schopler, 1998; Koudenburg et al, 2017), by building common ground. As Koudenburg et al (2017: 50) argue, this establishing of a common ground 'includes the implicit notion that viewpoints are shared among a collective, and therefore signals the existence of a we'. The greater a sense of rapport two people share, the more they'll feel part of a 'we'. Intuitively, the greater the common ground, and the greater the sense of being a 'we', the easier communication will be. It takes less effort to perspective-take (or *mind-read*), because our perspectives are already quite close.

At a more granular level, the behavioural coordination and synchrony that often scaffolds rapport-building is sometimes described as *interpersonal attunement* (we'll see more of this later, e.g. in Chapter 7). Synchronising or attuning with others, by virtue of spontaneous actions such as aligning with another's body language (e.g. adopting another's mannerisms or falling into step with your walking partner) or spoken language provides the building blocks for much of human communication: from our early language acquisition through to trust-building and deep, embodied, mutual understanding.

In the next chapter, we'll take a look at what some linguists have to say about finding common ground and reaching mutual understanding, and how we might explain why sometimes it's really easy, yet sometimes really difficult, to understand what people mean by what they say.

Chapter 3: Making sense in a complex world

'...what words mean is a matter of what people mean by them.'
(Grice, 1989: 340)

Zoltar's riddle

When I was a child, we had a family ritual that we'd undertake several times each summer. We drive down to a local coastal town, have a picnic of warm marmite sandwiches and Hula Hoop crisps on a pebbly beach then wrap up the event with a visit to the arcades on a nearby pier. Our parents would give me and my sister £2.50 'silly money' each, which we would change down into small coins held in a paper cup and we would proceed to entertain ourselves for the next hour frittering them into the mechanical mouths of machines. The arcades were bright and noisy, but consistently so, and familiar. I would allow the flashing neon lights and loud honks, the high-pitched bells and the manic chittering of the machines to merge with the waves lapping beneath us and to lull me into a state of suspended animation. I'd push copper two-pence pieces into the thick slots of my chosen machine in time with its regular mechanical breathing, swaying with it, and let the endlessly falling shiny things purify my insides in what, I see retrospectively, was an autistic flow state.

My sister was different. She'd begin with me on the two-penny machines but would soon become bored, and race excitedly from grabber-machine to fruit-machine, to shoot-em-ups to the race-car simulator.

Her favourite above all, however, was Zoltar the Fortune Teller. An austere and imposing (to a small child), life-sized animatronic figure, he sat inside his esoterically decorated glass booth, staring stoically ahead. He was pricey, but he paid dividends. Once the coins had landed he would lurch into his prophetic performance, and as a parting gift, your fortune would emerge on a small paper ticket. One particular pilgrimage to the oracle yielded the following message:

'Don't worry about going bald!'

***

How would you interpret such a message, presented to you on a small slip of paper, purportedly by a being that can see into your future? As with most utterances, there are several possibilities, some of which might include the following:

- Going bald is not something for you to be concerned about (as it will never happen).
- Stop worrying about going bald (because you have worse things to worry about).
- You are going to go bald, but it won't be so bad. Let it happen and don't fear it.

The problem with language and words is that it often all comes down to interpretation…

Meaning and implied meaning

The study of meaning (semantics) and meaning or language use in context (pragmatics) are vast fields with long histories: fascinating, but too vast and long to cover in depth here. However, in order to best contextualise and understand the foundations of *relevance theory* (to come, later in this chapter), and how that, in turn, might help us better understand breakdowns in cross-neurotype communication, we first need to make a short diversion around the idea of *meaning* and *implied meaning*.

Some communication, as we saw in the last chapter, can be easily described as code-based. Information is coded into a signal and decoded by the receiver. A bee does a waggle dance with her body oriented at a certain angle to the sun, at a certain tempo, and her sisters understand directly where to travel to find the nectar described. It might be tempting to think that all words function this way – definitions can be looked up in dictionaries and (encoded) meanings can be determined. But as I'm sure many of us know only too well, words don't always mean what they mean. Or, as philosopher of language Paul Grice (1989: 340) once said: 'What words mean is a matter of what people mean by them'.

Grice was a linguist most interested in the field of pragmatics – the study of how meaning works in context. He wanted to try to find an explanation for why it might be, if meaning is coded and static, that conversational communication sometimes fails. Within pragmatics, the basic idea is that the context of any given *utterance* (the broad term for vocalised communicative behaviour) sometimes subtly but sometimes dramatically influences how the utterance is understood: or, *interpreted*. For most human-language interactions, it seems essential to, first, (semantically) decode (i.e. identify the agreed dictionary definition meaning) and, second, (pragmatically) infer a speaker's *implied meaning*. In other words, there are two layers of meaning: the directly communicated layer (that the dictionary will be able to give you), and the indirectly communicated layer (what someone is additionally *implying*). This – particularly to an autistic person who likes rules, straight-talking, and simplicity – sounds like an absolute chaotic nightmare, so let's take some deep breaths and unpack it a little more…

Two types of meaning

A slight digression (but hopefully an interesting one) en route to understanding these parallel layers of directly communicated and indirectly communicated meaning is Grice's deep-dive into what it means to 'mean' something. This is the kind of profound philosophical question you might find yourself pondering deep in the night when you can't sleep, but Grice tried to tackle it tidily with logic and linguistics.

In short, Grice identified that there are two quite different ways in which the word 'means' can be used.

1. What Grice called **natural meaning**:

   > Your car has been left unused through winter and you're finally getting back in to drive it but you're worried the battery might have gone flat. You put the key tentatively in the ignition and turn. The engine starts. The engine starting **means** the battery isn't flat.

   In the case of 'natural meaning', something in the world (the engine starting) allows us to infer that something else (the battery not being flat) must be the case.

2. What Grice called **non-natural meaning**:

   > You're riding the bus home and you hear a ding of the bell. The dinging of the bell **means** that someone wants to get off at the next stop.

   In the case of 'non-natural meaning', intentions of some sort are involved. Imagine, if you will, your ungainly autistic author with poor proprioception who stumbles over her own feet in a cafe and, putting her hand out to steady herself, finds it in the lap of an unexpected stranger. The awkward and rapid explanation 'I didn't mean to do that!' could easily be replaced with 'I didn't intend to do that'. In the example above, the sound of the bell 'means' that some other passenger has pressed the bell with the intention of alerting the driver of their wish to disembark.

Grice's thinking about meaning introduced the idea of *intentional* communication and created the springboard for an *inferential model* of language: an alternative to the code model we saw earlier.

An inferential model of communication: intentions and ostension

For Grice's 'non-natural meaning' – the one that involves intentions rather than the drawing of conclusions from simple evidence, like the ignition starting meaning the battery isn't dead – there was something important about the addressee recognising the speaker's intention to communicate something (the passenger ringing the bell).

Communication that is both intentional and overt is called ostensive communication. Let's take an example. Imagine you're sitting around a table with a friend and an open bottle of wine. Your glass is empty and you're ready for more. You might simply place your glass within your friend's eyeline, intending for them to notice and offer you another. In this case, while you did seek to benefit from their natural predisposition to make relevant inferences (*the glass is empty, they might want a top-up*), the communicative action would not count as *ostensive* because you didn't make your intention to communicate your desire for a top-up clear. Should you wish to make your desire for wine known, you might waggle your glass, give a little wink or (if you've already had a few) bark 'TOP ME UP!' In other words: provide an *ostensive stimulus*. An ostensive stimulus, in essence, is really just some action that claims another's attention: a wave, a polite but communicative cough, a scream or some spoken words.

Within the inferential model, human communication is seen to revolve around the producing and interpreting of evidence (of intentions), achieved by the use of an ostensive stimulus. In *ostensive-inferential communication* (to use its full title), two intentions are understood to be in play with each utterance. The first, the *informative intention*, is to inform the addressee of something (*I'd like some more wine*). The second, the *communicative intention*, is to inform the addressee of your informative intention (*I'm making it clear to you that I would like some more wine*). In reality, the very act of vocalising something, or uttering it ostensively (waggling the glass and giving a little wink) usually makes the first informative intention (*that I'd like some more wine*) evident, thus fulfilling both.

This idea of intentional communication helps to explain that second layer of implied meaning. *Implications* (in the technical, pragmatic sense) are what you might logically draw as conclusions from certain information or premises. By their nature, they're indirect information that require inference to arrive at. *Implicatures*, on the other hand, are the intentionally communicated implications. They're part of the informative intention, but delivered indirectly. For example. If you offer me a coffee at 5pm, I'll likely answer that 'coffee keeps me awake'. There are a number of potential implications here, including two opposing ones: *I don't want to drink coffee because it will keep me awake* and *I do want to drink coffee because I'd like to stay awake.* If you ask me this at the end of a working day when I'm getting into hygge-inducing pyjamas, the implicature is likely that I do not want a coffee because it will keep me awake and I'm nestling down. If you're offering me a 5pm coffee before I set off for a long evening drive, the implicature (the indirectly communicated implication that I would like you to derive, and will assume you will derive) is that, yes, I would like a coffee, as this will help to keep me awake and alert on the road.

Communication as a cooperative affair

The final piece of the puzzle, and the contribution for which Grice is perhaps most well-known, is his *Cooperative Principle*. Wanting to explain how people might be arriving at these implicatures (the indirect, implied meanings) from the utterances they hear, Grice (1975) proposed that communication is in fact a cooperative affair, involving interlocutors (people engaged in communication with one another) who are (more or less) equally invested in communicative success. So far, so fair. Speakers want to be understood by the people they're speaking to, he argued, and will shape what they say to best make that happen. From the listener's perspective, once an ostensive stimulus is identified, it would be reasonable to assume that the speaker will be trying to meet certain communicative standards. Grice thought that, as such, we all follow a kind of communication pact – the *Cooperative Principle* – driven by rational principles that he titled *maxims of conversation*:

- **Cooperative Principle:** Make your conversation contribution such as is required, at the stage at which it occurs, by the accepted purpose or direction of the talk exchange in which you are engaged.
- **Maxim of Quantity:**
  i. (Make your contribution as informative as is required (for the current purposes of the exchange).
  ii. Do not make your contribution more informative than is required.
- **Maxim of Quality:**
  i. Do not say what you believe to be false.
  ii. Do not say that for which you lack adequate evidence.
- **Maxim of Relation:**
  i. Be relevant.

- **Maxim of Manner:**
    i. Avoid obscurity of expression.
    ii. Avoid ambiguity.
    iii. Be brief (avoid unnecessary prolixity[15]).
    iv. Be orderly.

(Grice, 1975a: 45- 46)

There are, of course, some potential issues with the above, including the fact that these maxims are most certainly culturally-dependent and Euro-centric. What *was* and remains useful though, is the idea that communication is, according to Grice, ultimately a collaborative and cooperative act. Speakers wish for their communication to be successful, and will construct their utterances in accordance with the (culturally-agreed) principles and maxims that will support this. Crucially, so long as speakers are following the Cooperative Principle, their utterances will, at some level, *be relevant*. And (and this is where we start to tie things together) if a relevant meaning is not obvious from that first layer of linguistically encoded meaning, listeners will assume an extra layer of indirectly expressed meaning and seek out the relevant implicature.

Returning to the Zoltar/baldness example for one moment; the problem for my sister, then, was that she was not dealing with a living, breathing fortune-teller but an automated facsimile. Unfortunately for her, she was too young to make this distinction. With limited additional information about the 'speaker' available, isolating the correct interpretation (or implicature) of his warning (*don't worry about going bald!*) fell to plain-old panicked guesswork. Zoltar, despite her pawing at the glass and pleading, remained decidedly uncooperative. For my sister, the outcome of this guesswork led to lifelong phalacrophobia (fear of going bald)…

If you've followed this far (well done!), you may be wondering what exactly 'being relevant' (and being *obviously* relevant) in Grice's above maxims might mean. If so, you're asking the right questions (and even Grice himself acknowledged that this area of his theory could benefit from some further development). How do we, as listeners, so frequently arrive at the correct implicatures (implied meanings) and, as speakers, ensure that this might be so? The question isn't so much 'why does communication sometimes fail?' – as Grice had asked himself – but more

---

15 LOL, Grice, read the room…

'how does it ever succeed when the scope of possible interpretation is infinite?' Enter, stage right, Dan Sperber and Deirdre Wilson, with their perfectly titled (and central to this book) *relevance theory*.

Relevance Theory

> *'There is a point where too much information and too much information processing can hurt. Cognition is the art of focusing on the relevant and deliberately ignoring the rest.'*
>
> (Gigerenzer & Todd, 1999: 21)

Sperber and Wilson (1986/1995) took Grice's philosophical groundwork as a starting point and applied knowledge from (the then quite novel) cognitive science discoveries to try to provide an answer to the question: how do we determine what is relevant (when constructing and interpreting utterances)? There is a lot that can be said about relevance theory, enough to fill a whole book. Indeed, if it tickles your interest, I can highly recommend Billy Clark's primer *Relevance Theory*, which breaks down in detail some of the more nuanced aspects of its approach to utterance interpretation and the nitty-gritty of implicatures, communicative intentions and the suchlike. For the purpose of this book, however, the basics will do, which we'll explore below.

One of the issues that most puzzled Sperber and Wilson, was how it is that – usually, or certainly more often than not – we tend to draw the correct inferences and arrive at the correct implicatures when there are so many possible variables. Grice had suggested it had something to do with speakers being bound to follow the Cooperative Principle and conversational maxims (be truthful, appropriately informative, relevant, and formulate your utterance in the appropriate manner). If listeners can assume speakers will be abiding by these maxims, they can be guided towards correct implicatures where utterances appear to diverge from them.

Sperber and Wilson, in turn, take a more cognitive approach. Their central claim, and the claim at the heart of relevance theory, is that 'the expectations of relevance raised by an utterance are precise and predictable enough to guide the hearer toward the speaker's meaning' (Wilson & Sperber, 2004: 607). Importantly, this expectation arises 'because the search for relevance is a basic feature of human cognition, which communicators may exploit' (Wilson & Sperber, 2004: 608). They take the starting point that in a densely information-rich world, with limited processing power available at any given moment, our minds have surely evolved to be economical with what we pay our attention to. Too much information to process in one go can hurt: something autistic people may be especially familiar with. In order to achieve this economy of focus, our rational inferencing processes – the way in which our minds draw meaning from the facts and world around us – must involve some kind of 'fast and frugal heuristics' (Gigerenzer & Todd, 1999), i.e. rules for cognitive processing shortcuts. The first of relevance theory's two key principles, the Cognitive Principle of Relevance, is a suggestion for how this may work generally, but particularly so in the domain of ostensive-inferential communication.

The Cognitive Principle of Relevance

Consider the following. Imagine this person is at a dinner party at a friend's house and they say 'It's getting a bit chilly'. The explicitly communicated meaning here (linguistically encoded) is that the temperature is dropping to a point where it has become noticeably cool. But what is the purpose of the utterance? It could simply be to share an observation, but there is also a whole range of potential implicatures – indirectly communicated meanings – that this speaker may have intended their addressee to understand. Herein lies the nightmare: how do we know what anyone means, when speakers could mean lots of different things with what they say?

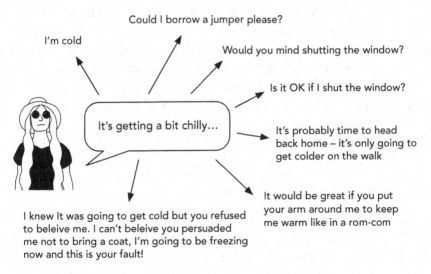

Figure 2: Seven potential interpretations of a single utterance.

The Cognitive Principle of Relevance definitively places the search for relevance at the centre of both human cognition (remember those 'fast and frugal heuristics'?) and, more specifically, utterance interpretation. According to relevance theory, in order to determine whether something is relevant or not – and thus whether it merits our most precious commodity: our attention – we have developed a quick, shorthand formula by which to calculate it.

For any new input, a balance is weighed up between the cognitive effort required to process it and the potential value it brings. An input is considered to be relevant when its processing, within the available context, produces some positive *cognitive effect*, i.e. 'a worthwhile difference to the individual's representation of the world' (Wilson & Sperber, 2004: 608). Cognitive effects are quite technically defined by Sperber and Wilson but essentially include any changes to current understanding, any new facts or beliefs, or any strengthening or contradicting of existing beliefs or assumptions.

In the case of the above dinner party, it is perhaps so that the speaker can see, clearly, that a window is open. Next to the window, they can see their friend, who can also see that the window is open. Perhaps the friend has earlier expressed a concern that this person was looking a little poorly and was worried they were coming down with a bug. By uttering 'It's getting a bit chilly' in this context, the most relevant implicature is likely (to the friend by the window): 'Would you mind shutting the window?'

It is not, of course, simply a question of whether something is or isn't relevant. At any given moment there will be any amount of potentially relevant information available in our sensory-perceptual field, and any number of potentially relevant interpretations of an utterance. As a property, relevance is measured by degree, and as a guiding principle for utterance interpretation, by finding the sweet spot between the least cognitive efforts made for the greatest cognitive effects gained. Or, as Sperber and Wilson themselves put it:

Sperber and Wilson's recipe for relevance:

'a. Other things being equal, the greater the positive cognitive effects achieved by processing an input, the greater the relevance of the input to the individual at that time.

b. *Other things being equal, the greater the processing effort expended, the lower the relevance of the input to the individual at that time.'*

(Wilson & Sperber, 2004: 609)

For the dinner party example, any (or indeed several) of the potential implicatures may be relevant, but in that particular context, the inference that the speaker would like the window shut, please, lands most effortlessly in the sweet spot between spending time and energy considering other possible interpretations and arriving at some new, relevant information.

The Communicative Principle of Relevance (and being a 'helpful speaker')

The second principle on which relevance theory is based – the Communicative Principle of Relevance – is where things start to get juicier. This says that *because* human cognition is geared to the search for relevance, speakers ensure that their utterances are shaped to make the most of that. This, in turn, means that hearers can trust that what's being said to them is relevant enough to be worth the processing effort required to understand it. Let's dig into this a little more.

According to relevance theory, any ostensive stimulus carries with it a *presumption of optimal relevance* (Sperber & Wilson, 1986: 158), by virtue of the speaker bothering to utter something ostensively[16]. In providing such an ostensive stimulus, the speaker must believe it to be worth the processing effort of the intended receiver. The audience of an utterance may, as such, be entitled to expect this. Thus far, pretty logical. Speakers are seen to be intuitively crafting their utterances according to the principles of relevance, to the best of their abilities and on the best knowledge they have available of the intended addressee and of the shared context. Wilson and Sperber (2004: 612) summarise these principles as follows:

---

16 In Chapter 5, we will revisit this idea of ostensive communication carrying a presumption of optimal relevance in the context of echolalia and other typically autistic communicative behaviours that were, historically (and I would say wrongly), considered meaningless.

Communicative Principle of Relevance

Every ostensive stimulus conveys a presumption of its own optimal relevance.

Presumption of optimal relevance

a. The ostensive stimulus is relevant enough to be worth the audience's processing effort.

b. It is the most relevant one compatible with communicator's abilities and preferences.

Just as with Grice's Cooperative Principle, the expectation is that communicators wish to be helpful to those with whom they are communicating. Some studies, including one by relevance theorist Dan Sperber and colleagues (Van Der Henst et al, 2002) do seem to show that even strangers (with therefore no vested interest in being liked or pleasing their interlocutor) will adjust their utterances in order to make them *optimally relevant*. For example, usually, when asked for the time, a 'helpful speaker' will usually round their answer rather than provide the precise minute (i.e. 10.40 rather than 10.37). The reason for this, the researchers suggest, is that speakers 'are always trying to achieve relevance to their hearer' (Van Der Henst et al, 2002: 457), and as such will offer an answer that may allow the hearer to derive the relevant information with as little processing effort as possible (a rounded number requires less processing effort that specific one). However, when the time was requested along with a declaration of an impending appointment, the closer the minute of the appointment time, the less rounding that took place. From this, the authors concluded that speakers were considering the needs of the asker, and providing more precise answers when it could reasonably be inferred that this information was pertinent.

Cognitive environments and manifestness

One further, and really important, feature central to relevance theory is the notion of 'cognitive environments'. Every individual is understood to possess their own cognitive environment which is really the massing of all facts and assumptions both actually and *potentially* available to them in a given moment. This, then, includes all encyclopaedic knowledge, however presently or dimly accessible, and all permutations of that knowledge given the right context. For example, it is unlikely that a person would have it stored, as a distinct fact, that the King of England has never ridden a narwhal: this is a thought that most people would never have the need to entertain. However, should the topic arise (in one of those late-night, can't-sleep, ponderous conversations, or solo musings) an individual may well be able to generate this assumption based on their available knowledge and assumptions about the typical activities of British royalty and the wieldiness of narwhals. Within relevance theory, facts and assumptions that are *within potential reach* – reliant as they are on the precise combination of individual knowledge, cognitive abilities, and physical environment – are considered to be 'manifest'. In this instance, while it may well be that before reading the cursed sentences above you'd never conceived of Charles atop a horned marine beast, the idea (or *assumption* in relevance-theoretic terms) was nevertheless always manifest to you. Who knew?[17]

Cognitive environments, by their nature, are completely unique. The facts and assumptions that are available at any given moment to even two of the closest twin siblings, who share DNA and matching physical environments, will differ on account of their fluctuating cognitive abilities and different subjective experiences of the world. As Sperber and Wilson put it:

> 'Perceptual abilities vary in effectiveness from one individual to another. Inferential abilities also vary, and not just in effectiveness. People speak different languages, they have mastered different concepts; as a result, they can construct different representations and make different inferences.'
>
> (Sperber & Wilson, 1986: 38)

The ways in which the cognitive environments of people of differing neurotypes may diverge is something we'll be coming to in Chapter 3. But first, let's think about what happens when portions of two individual's cognitive environments do overlap.

---

17 And what other weird and wild assumptions might be lurking, manifest, at the edge of your consciousness?

Mutual cognitive environments and mutual manifestness

When portions of two individual's cognitive environments overlap, these shared facts and assumptions become what relevance theorists call a *mutual cognitive environment*. In many ways, a mutual cognitive environment is not dissimilar to what's described in everyday terms as 'common ground'. It may be that two individuals are currently within the same location (e.g. a classroom or park) and share the same physical environment, both able to see and experience similar things at the same time. It might be that they share autobiographical knowledge (they have the same friendship group, or work for the same organisation), or it may be that they share similar cultural experiences and knowledge of the world. Within a mutual cognitive environment, it is possible to both know (or potentially know) the same things at the same time, and here we're closing in on what is possibly the most important concept in relevance theory: *mutual manifestness*.

Where it is evident to two speakers that certain manifest (i.e., potentially accessible: like the king on a narwhal) facts or assumptions are shared, these facts and assumptions – which form the mutual cognitive environment – are said to be mutually manifest. For example, when I was a regular attendee of a local beekeeping club, I recognised that the other members likely had manifest to them (1) assumptions about pollen flow in our geographical region, at a particular time of year, and (2) that ivy blossom is a valuable source of nectar for honeybees as autumn unfolds in late September. When we meet together at the bee club, it's fair to take it that these assumptions are mutually manifest. On the other hand, my sister, albeit living in the same city, may not have these assumptions manifest to her on account of not being a hobbyist apiculturist.

When talking with my beekeeping companions during an uncharacteristically cold and wet September weekend, I could comfortably assume that the following utterance will carry a positive meaning that they will easily recognise:

'*My backyard is overgrown with ivy.*'

To my beekeeping pals, the most relevant implicature is that, although it is unseasonably cold, which might usually be a threat to a colony's ability to build enough stores for the upcoming winter, my backyard has plenty of potential sustenance so all is well. When talking with my sister, however, with whom the relevant facts and assumptions are not mutually manifest, the above utterance will carry a very different meaning. She will still assume that I have crafted my utterance so as to be optimally relevant and likely infer that my intended meaning was a complaint, perhaps that I wish to cut the pesky weed back, or perhaps, even, that I am asking to borrow some shears.

In order for something to be mutually manifest, it must meet two criteria. First, it must be manifest within the cognitive environment of both individuals and, second, both interlocutors must recognise that the fact or assumption is manifest to both themselves and the other. The concept of mutual manifestness is a little brain-bending to describe, but it's important because within the purview of relevance theory, it forms the basis from which judgements relating to the optimal relevance of an utterance are formed. You may recall that earlier we saw that speakers craft their utterances so as to be optimally relevant, to the best of their abilities and to the best knowledge they have available of the intended addressee and what is mutually manifest. What happens if these judgements about what is mutually manifest aren't accurate, perhaps due to your communication partner being of a different neurotype that you can't easily empathise with? We'll revisit this important question later, in Section 3.

Keep all this somewhere in the back of your cognitive environment, out of the way for now but within easy reach. In Section 2: Autistic meaning (and what do we mean by 'autism'?), we're taking a sidestep into the history of autism and autistic communicators. In the subsequent section, however, we'll return to what we've covered so far, and start to bring the two together: explaining how we might understand, in cognitive linguistic terms, the breakdowns in communication between autistic and non-autistic speakers using relevance theory. First, though, what *is* autism?

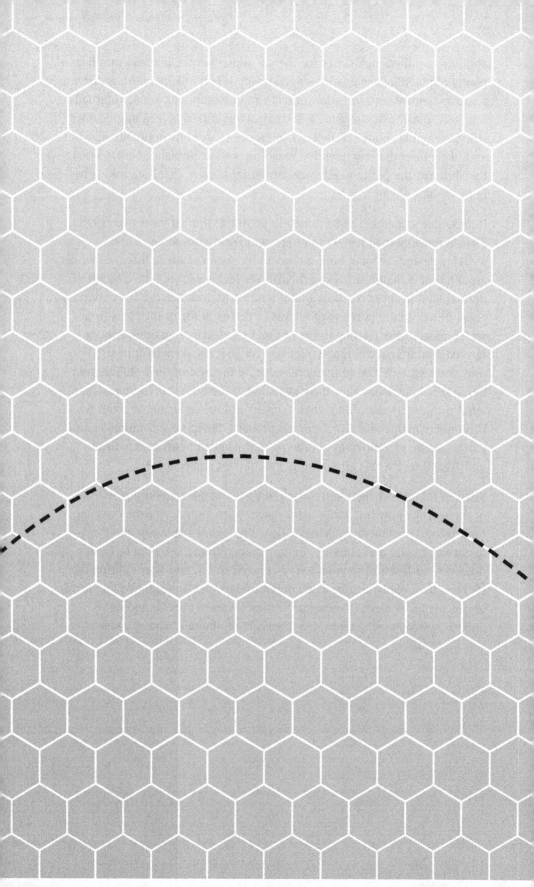

Section 2
Autistic Meaning (and what do we mean by 'autism'?)

Chapter 4: So, what *is* autism?

More big questions!

Before we can think in much detail about why communication sometimes falls short between autistic and non-autistic speakers, we need to have a clear sense of what exactly it is we mean when we say that someone is – or isn't – autistic.

However, as we'll see throughout this chapter, this isn't a completely simple matter. The construct of autism is now around 80-ish years old and yet we still don't have agreement across the social, medical and neuro-sciences about how autism should be defined, nor why some people are born autistic but others aren't. If you've picked up this book, you're probably already aware of some of the uncertainties and conflicts of opinion that abound the moment you start to talk about autism. Is autism, for instance, one distinct 'thing' (or, as I prefer, 'way of being') or is it a term given to many similar but slightly different 'things' (or ways of being)? Is it a disability, a disorder, an identity, or all three? Should we be looking for a cure (I don't think so, for the record) or should we be celebrating it?

This also makes it difficult when we try to talk about numbers of autistic people in the population. If you can't clearly define a thing, it's hard to measure it. Current estimates vary depending on what datasets are involved, but the range runs from the oft-quoted one in 100 (The NHS Information Centre, Brugha *et al*, 2012) to one in 36 (CDC, 2023): though neither of these figures is likely to properly represent the true picture. Often what is counted in these kinds of analyses is the number of people (or children, in the latter CDC example) who have autism diagnoses and – as we'll see in Chapter 10 – many autistic people face significant barriers to accessing formal diagnoses. This is especially the case for Black and Brown autistic people, for older autistic people, and for autistic women and girls. In the UK, waitlists for diagnostic assessments are often unconscionably long (Westminster Commission on Autism, 2021). Given these challenges and the stigma that still sometimes ensues following an autism diagnosis, many people simply choose not to pursue one.

While there *are* a lot of conflicting views about what autism is, they can broadly be divided into two categories: those that frame autism as a disorder (and that sit within what's known as *the medical model*), and those that see it as a difference (and sit more in a *social model of disability*). In this chapter, we'll skirt through the first – giving just enough information to provide a proper context – and linger on the second – honing in on the autistic-led theory of *monotropism* and the idea of the *sensory stranger*.

Just before we jump right in, however, let's first pause for a little tea[18].

There are autistic people *all over the world*. There are Asian autistic people, Black autistic people, Brown autistic people, and Indigenous autistic people. There are autistic people of all genders, all faiths, all sexualities and all ages. Not only does autism research have a race problem (Jones *et al*, 2020) – with the vast majority of research involving either exclusively white participants, an extremely high percentage of white participants, or simply not reporting racial demographics – the literature is highly Anglo-centric and the preponderance of published research is situated in the Global North. This, in part, reflects the way in which the English language dominates scholarly literature as well as the unequal funding and publishing structures globally: with fewer resources available to those in low- and middle-income countries. It also probably reflects the different ways that autism is interpreted in different cultures; what one culture might view as a neurodevelopmental disorder might be viewed by another as spirit possession, illness or a blessing (Grinker, 2016). As such, not all these different accounts and perspectives (yet) link up.

What is important to keep in mind for this chapter (and, to be fair, for the rest of the book), then, is that whenever something general is said about autism, it is important to take it with a little pinch of salt. Autism is a global phenomenon (as in, we autistic people are everywhere) but the scientific literature that often forms the basis of clinical descriptions of autism is very skewed towards a white, northern-hemisphere, Anglo-

---

18 By 'tea', here, I mean 'some hard truths' – but by all means, take this as a prompt for a tea break if you haven't hydrated for a while. You also might need a brew to hand: the first part of this chapter is a little hard-reading.

centric viewpoint. And with that caveat given, let's take a look at where the idea of 'autism' began...

The medical model: the naming and pathologising of a way of being

> 'Most of us have been trained to think about autism using a deficit model. Such a model, which focuses almost exclusively on impairments and limitations, ultimately leads us to see autistic individuals as broken people who are ill and, as my child's first psychologist explained, need to be fixed.'
>
> (Nicolaides, 2012: 503)

A very (very) brief history of a name

There is a lot that can be – and has been – said about the history and evolution of autism as an idea and a category[19]. The term 'autism' was first coined by a Swiss psychiatrist called Eugen Bleuler in 1911 in an attempt to categorise a specific type of childhood schizophrenia. From here it was next used by Grunya Efimovna Sukhareva in Russia in the early 1920s[20], then by Leo Kanner in America and Hans Asperger in Austria in the 1940s. All three were physicians treating young (and mostly male) children displaying unusual social behaviours and language. Forged within a pathologising psychiatric paradigm that focused on identifying and classifying impairments and deficits, 'autism' began its usage describing an aberrant and problematised way of being in the world. This has proven a difficult history to shake off.

The origins of the name and idea of 'autism' also have eugenicist associations. Most prominently, a recent review of previously unexplored archival documents (Czech, 2018) revealed the extent to which Hans Asperger was involved in National Socialist race hygiene policies under the nazi regime, including advocating for the forced sterilisation of autistic and other disabled individuals: a stance shared by Eugen Bleuler.

---

19 If you'd like read about this in more detail, try Steve Silberman's *Neurotribes*, or Bonnie Evans' *The metamorphosis of autism*.
20 Although this was largely forgotten for several decades until her work was later rediscovered (see Sher & Gibson, 2023).

Finally, it is of consequence that the first child patients on whom the category of autism was based, were largely (white, European) boys. The subsequent formalised diagnostic criteria became the determinants not only of who received the autism label, but also who was selected (or sought out) to participate as subjects in early autism research. Many of our foundational ideas about what autism does and doesn't entail are constrained by how young (white) boys of the time presented.

Measuring individuals against a 'mythical norm'

In the opening of her paper delivered at the Copeland Colloquium, Amherst College, 1980, Audre Lorde (1984: 114) had the following to say:

> *'Much of Western European history conditions us to see human differences in simplistic opposition to each other: dominant/ subordinate, good/bad, up/down, superior/inferior. In a society where the good is defined in terms of profit rather than in terms of human need, there must always be some group of people who, through systematised oppression, can be made to feel surplus, to occupy the place of the dehumanised inferior.'*

The focus of Lorde's address was on the cruelty of a capitalist society towards people who find themselves designated as 'different'. For Lorde, this talk was particularly pertinent for Black women in the USA (where she was speaking), who faced – and continue to face – systemic racism and sexism. However, her argument was intended for all those who fall short of what she referred to as the 'mythical norm', i.e. 'white, thin, male, young, heterosexual, Christian, and financially secure' (*Ibid*).

Talking about when the deviation from the (mythical) norm is a disability of some kind, Erickson (2014: 13) reminds us that:

> *'So called "truths" about disabled people are informed by a long history of medical, charity and eugenic models of disability which take up disability, and particular bodies and/or minds, as being in a state of biomedical malfunction. This understanding constructs our needs, lives and desires as outside normativity and therefore unintelligible.'*

For a long time, autism was seen in a wholly negative light, as a deviance from the (mythical) norm of a 'healthy' body-mind. As a result, considerable research effort has been put into divining its cause so that it might be both treated and, ultimately, eradicated. As a consequence, historically – but even today in some fields of autism research – research findings have often been interpreted through a deficit-focused lens 'as low-level by-products of high-level deficits, not as direct manifestations of intelligence' (Dawson et al, 2007: 657). For example, Morsanyi et al (2009) conducted a study to test how autistic adolescents would perform compared to neurotypical teenagers on a set of tests that measure cognitive bias when using reasoning skills. Participants undertook three famous tasks from biases and heuristics literature (the '*conjunction fallacy*' and two versions of the '*engineers and lawyers problem*'). The researchers found that – as predicted – the autistic participants were, in fact, *less susceptible* to cognitive biases: i.e. they made fewer reasoning errors due to biases in their thinking than the non-autistic participants. However, the researchers concluded not that autistic people may have an advantage in avoiding cognitive bias in these situations, but that their deficits in contextual processing must be impeding their ability to compute the potential biases...

From within this deficit-focused, medical model, there have been a large number of theories proposed as explanations of and for autism. There are too many to cover here and they're not really the focus of this book. However, many comprehensive overviews already exist should you wish to dig deeper[21]. Of the medical model theories that have stuck, three in particular have come to monopolise the discourse. Because of their dominance in how autism is understood around the world, they're worth summarising before we move on to more humane framings that better align with the spirit of this book.

Suggested 'deficits' in theory of mind

One of the most pervasive stereotypes shaping how autistic people are understood is that autistic people lack empathy, and struggle to understand the perspectives or feelings of others. This has its roots in early autism research, beginning in the early 1980s, that used the Sally-Anne task and

---

[21] I can highly recommend Nick Chown's *Understanding and Evaluating Autism Theory* (2017) as a great autistic-written text, or Sue Fletcher-Watson and Francesa Happé's *Autism: A new introduction to psychological theory and current debate* (2019).

other similar experiments to test the hypothesis that autistic children[22] lacked theory of mind. In one now-seminal study, researchers Baron-Cohen, Leslie and Frith (1985: 38, 43) explained that autistic children's 'range of socially impaired behaviour: from total withdrawal through passivity to repetitive pestering', their 'low level of social competence, even in able autistic children' and their tendency to 'treat people and objects alike' was due to their inability to 'impute beliefs to others … [or]… predict the behaviour of other people'.

Recall from our earlier meeting with the theory of mind concept that Baron-Cohen, the lead researcher on this project[23], went on to say that theory of mind is the 'quintessential ability that makes us human' (Baron-Cohen, 2001: 174). There is something deeply dehumanising in saying, 'so, there's this *thing* that makes us humans human, but *this* group of humans evidently don't have it, because they behave differently'; particularly when (as we saw in Chapter 2) various non-human animals are also believed to possess some theory of mind skills. However, to cut some slack, the field has moved on a lot since these early studies. At the time of this and similar studies, researchers believed autism to be 'a rare condition, affecting about four in every 10,000 children' (*Ibid*). It was also believed that the majority of autistic children had what would now be understood to be co-occurring learning difficulties. It is pretty fair to say that the participants included in these early studies weren't particularly representative of autistic people as we understand autism today.

Suggested 'weak central coherence'

The theory of mind deficit theory of autism seemed highly convincing at the time and, indeed, its legacy remains dominant in autism discourse today. One of its great selling points was that it appeared to provide an explanation for many of the difficulties autistic children seemed to experience in the three core areas that formed the autism label: i.e. in imagination, sociality and communication. However, some of the 'non-triad' features of the autistic profile remained unaccounted for and while the theory of mind deficit explanation had been readily accepted, researchers were aware that 20 percent of autistic participants *did* pass the false belief task in the original Baron-Cohen, Leslie and Frith experiment

---

[22] Strange as it may seem now, at the time of these studies, no-one really spoke about autistic adults.
[23] …and many subsequent discourse-shaping studies, who was given a knighthood in 2021 for his 'services to people with autism'…

(1985), and 36 percent in a later follow-up study (Leslie & Frith, 1988). Responding to these concerns, Frith and Happé (1994) proposed a possible, additional cognitive deficit that might explain these peripheral anomalies: the theory of weak central coherence.

They had noticed that among those features of autism not explained by a (supposed) inability to mentalise (e.g. restricted and repetitive interests; a need for sameness; islets of ability; savant skills; excellent rote memory…) there was a root tendency towards detail-orientation. Typical information processing, they argued, features a 'tendency to draw together diverse information to construct higher-level meaning in context': a drive towards what they termed 'central coherence' (Frith & Happé, 1994: 121). Cognition, in this framework, is a gist-finding exercise whereby a holistic overview is prioritised above costly attention to the detail of smaller parts. Information is processed in context, with the initial search directed toward global, rather than local, meaning. For autistic people, it was suggested that there was 'a core deficit in central processing resulting in failure to extract global form/meaning' (Happé & Frith, 2006).

One key piece of research that inspired this theory was Shah and Frith's (1983) 'Children's Embedded Figures Test'. In this experiment, the autistic children were significantly more competent at identifying the hidden shape within a complex picture than chronologically and mentally age-matched neurotypical children, and also 'showed qualitatively different strategies' (1983: 619) in achieving the task.

The original proponents of the theory, Happé and Frith, have since stepped back a little from the strong claims of weak central coherence theory, following a literature review of over a decade's worth of empirical research investigating central coherence in cognition (Happé & Frith, 2006). They revised the theory to instead describe a bias towards local processing in autism – as opposed to a deficit in global processing abilities – with the acknowledgement that as well as difficulties in some areas, this processing style may also bring unique strengths and talents. Indeed, in a more recent study by Swettenham *et al* (2014), the researchers found that the autistic tendency towards detail-oriented attention helped make them less susceptible to something called 'inattention blindness'[24]. Participants were presented with a series of crosses on a computer screen, each for

---

24 When people fail to notice a conspicuous visual event because they are focused on something else: for example, missing seeing a man dressed in a gorilla suit walking through the middle of a basketball game because they are busy counting passes of the ball.

a short time, and asked to identify which of the two lines (the vertical or the horizontal) was longer. During this activity, an unexpected shape appeared briefly in a peripheral location on the screen. In one condition, the lines were easy to differentiate, and in another, the lines were more similar in length. The autistic children in this study outperformed the non-autistic matched controls in both conditions: both in the number of correct answers they gave about differences in line lengths, and in noticing the surprise shape and being able to report back on its colour, shape and location correctly. A cognitive style that privileges detail over gist may create some problems, but it does also have its benefits.

Suggested executive functioning difficulties

Of the three main deficits-based, cognitive theories of autism, executive functioning theory is perhaps of least relevance to our discussion of cross-neurotype communication, but it deserves a brief mention if only on account of its enduring presence. Executive function is a slightly loose umbrella term used to describe a suite of cognitive functions such as working memory, impulse control, formation of abstract concepts, planning, task-switching and the starting and finishing of actions (Chown, 2016; Hill, 2004). What unites these functions is their role in a kind of 'cognitive oversight mode' of behaviour. Autistic people, people with ADHD, people with Tourette's Syndrome and those who have experienced frontal lobe damage have seemed to exhibit impairments or difficulties in various executive functioning skills (Happé et al, 2006; Hill, 2004).

A number of experiments devised to measure different executive functioning abilities (such as the famous *Tower of Hanoi/Tower of London* test for planning and *The Wisconsin Card Sorting Test* for mental flexibility) have generated mixed results over the years (see: Happé et al, 2006; Hill, 2004; Milton, 2012a). As difficulties with some executive functioning skills cannot be said to be specific to autism, as a theory of autism, it only has limited reach. Anecdotal evidence from autistic people themselves certainly supports the idea that switching attention (at speed) can be problematic (Milton, 2012a). However, the autistic-led theory of *monotropism* (see below) may explain this – and many of the other difficulties thought of as executive function impairments – equally as well.

The medical model: in summary

Explanations of autism based on cognitive impairments dominated how autism and autistic people were understood for a long time. Yet the 'prominence and the consensus on the potential explanatory value' of these previously promising cognitive theories have begun to decline in the past decade' (Lord *et al*, 2020: 4). In addition to them often lacking specificity for autism, they are 'largely non-developmental, applying only to a single point in time' (*Ibid*). One criticism in particular that can be levelled at all three of the above theories is that they each can only partially explain some autistic traits. Most importantly, 'they show little concern for the embodiment and situatedness of the autistic person...' nor the way in which interactive factors play an explanatory role in social difficulties with others (De Jaegher, 2013: 3).

The erasure of the bodily experience of what it is to be autistic within autism theory is a thread that has often been taken up by autistic writers and self-advocates (e.g. Yergeau, 2017). And yet as we saw at the start of this book, in order to understand any cognising living being, we need to think about its body as its primary, interactional interface with its environment. How a being is embodied in the world shapes how it experiences it. I think it would be fair to say, then, that any theory of the mind without a footing in the body is an incomplete one.

The social model: autism as a minority neurotype

> '[Autistic people] are not disordered (the irony with the term being that so many people with autism are highly ordered in their thinking), nor should we automatically dismiss developmental differences as impairments. Certainly the neurological complexities can be baffling to the neurotypical – as, equally, the neurotypical world is baffling to the [autistic person]. This does not make either or both populations disordered – simply, different.'
> (Beardon, 2007: para.5)

We find ourselves amid a sea change in autism research. Over the past three decades, interest in autism as a field of research has boomed

(Pellicano, 2014) and along with the dramatic increase in the volume of studies investigating different aspects of the autistic experience, a shift has begun in terms of how autism is defined (Happé & Frith, 2020). Under the medical model, autism was (and still is) seen as a deviation from a 'normal', healthy body-mind, rooted in a deficit narrative that focused on impairments. Now, thanks to the advocacy and hard work of members of the disability rights movement and autistic advocate-activists, an alternative view exists in the mainstream that frames autism as a type of difference[25].

The social model of disability (Oliver, 1983) flips the focus from individual experiences of impairment to a collective experience of disablement. Developed by disabled people themselves, disability is positioned as something that happens within the interaction of an individual and their environment. It doesn't ignore or undermine the pain (both physical and mental) that often comes with being disabled or experiencing disabling conditions, but the disablement itself is understood to come from the barriers that exist within the world around them. Barriers might be physical (e.g. lack of access to wheelchair-friendly toilets), social (e.g. dehumanising assumptions about capacity or ability), cultural (e.g. absence of signers or closed captions for Deaf attendees of an event) or financial (e.g. services that are prohibitively expensive to those reliant of disability benefits).

Autism as a (minority) neurotype

The social model of disability sets the scene for approaches to understanding autism that take a difference-not-deficit approach. Aligned with the social model of disability is the concept of *neurodiversity* – a term that has become far more commonly known in the last few years. Making reference to the term *biodiversity*, 'neurodiversity' holds the idea that it is normal and natural for there to be a diversity of different kinds of minds and different types of cognitive processing within the human species. The neurodiversity paradigm evolved out of the burgeoning autism-rights

---

[25] You may have noticed that I fall short, here, of writing that autism is a form of 'neurological difference'. Autism is categorised as a neurodevelopmental condition, medically, and we have a common conception in (Global Northern) society now that autistic people are 'wired differently'. I like this metaphor, in some ways, as it communicates the idea that different wirings of brains exist and are acceptable (rather than faulty). That said, I'm not sure brains and cognition are quite as simple as a mechanical, computer-based metaphor suggests. I'm also not sure that autism can be perfectly explained by how our brains and nervous systems are. I prefer to think about autism as a *way of being* (Fein, 2018; Sinclair, 1993) in the sense that Thomas Nagel (1974) thought about *what it is like to be* a particular kind of being – but more about Nagel in Chapter 8.

movement that saw autistic activists connect as a community in the early 1990s across online discussion boards (Walker, 2021) and came as a counter to an increasingly vocal, 'autism-parent' lobby demanding a cure for their child's autism (Robertson & Ne'eman, 2008). In xyr[26] now-seminal speech given at the 1993 International Conference on Autism in Toronto entitled Don't Mourn for Us, autistic activist Jim Sinclair intreated parents of autistic children to:

> '...*take a moment to consider it: Autism is a way of being. It is not possible to separate the person from the autism. Therefore, when parents say, I wish my child did not have autism, what they're really saying is, I wish the autistic child I have did not exist, and I had a different (non-autistic) child instead.*'
>
> (Sinclair, 1993)

The neurodiversity paradigm fundamentally challenges the premise that there's only one normal or healthy type of brain (or mind or way of being...) and acknowledges the diversity of ways in which neurological difference[27] might manifest. The neurodiversity movement (a social justice movement founded in the neurodiversity paradigm – Walker, 2021) argues for full societal inclusion, equality and respect for those who are neurodivergent (in other words, anyone who isn't neurotypical). It's important to say, here, that while neurodiversity proponents do advocate for neurodivergences to be 'seen not as pathologies needing a cure, but as natural differences which should be accepted and accommodated' (Graby, 2015: 233), it doesn't entail that people don't sometimes need help, or that being autistic or otherwise neurodivergent can't sometimes be disabling.

Minority stress

There are, of course, inherent challenges to being a minority neurotype (anyone who is neurodivergent – including people with ADHD, Tourettes, dyslexia, dyspraxia, dyscalculia and many other neurodivergent ways of being) living in a neurotypically-dominant world that come in addition to any innate neurotype-specific differences. Not only is society generally not set up to accommodate disabled and neurodivergent people's needs, but the burden of constantly coming up against societal barriers and social

---

26 'xyr' is a gender neutral pronoun that Jim Sinclair uses, similar to 'their'.
27 See Note 8, above, about the neurological basis of difference.

prejudice can have a deleterious effect on one's well-being. In contrast to the medical model's pathologisation of autistic experiences and ways of processing, the autistic rights and neurodiversity movements argue that it is in fact the routine marginalisation, stigma and exclusion of autistic people 'that thwart the wellbeing and functioning of Autistics' (Chapman & Carel, 2022: 619). It is the experience of living in a world that doesn't accommodate your differences, and judges you cruelly, that creates a lot of the challenges that can come with being autistic (we'll revisit this more in Chapter 9).

Autistic scholar Monique Botha (Botha, 2020; Botha & Frost, 2020) has turned to the *minority stress* model to explain this impact. The minority stress model aims to explain the evident health disparities that exist between stigmatised minority groups as contrasted with majority groups:

> *'Researchers hypothesize that decreased social standing leads to stigmatized minority groups being exposed to more stressful life situations, with simultaneously fewer resources to cope with these events. Social structure facilitates this process through acts of discrimination and social exclusion, which are added stress burdens that socially advantaged groups are not equally exposed to.'*
>
> (Botha & Frost 2020: 22)

As we'll see in Chapter 9, autistic people face a shocking health gap, both in terms of physical and mental health as well as life expectancy. They also face significant barriers to equitable education, financial stability and employment (Grant *et al*, 2023): all things that support individuals to thrive. It is very likely that many of the social, mental and physical challenges autistic people experience result directly from the struggle to flourish (as a neuro-minority) in a hostile and inhospitable (neurotypical and stigmatising) environment.

Sensory strangers[28]

> *'What is an autistic body? As an autistic person, I am well aware of the ways in which my "neurological disorder" manifests itself in*

---

[28] To borrow a very good term from the title of Jackson-Perry, Rosqvist, Annable and Kourti's equally good chapter 'Sensory strangers: Travels in normate sensory worlds', in *Neurodiversity studies: A new critical paradigm*.

and through my muscles and sinew, the ways in which autism rolls off my tongue, transforms my gait into autly bounce, stiffens the contours of my face as my eyes survey a room. Autism is embodied; my embodiment is autism.

(Yergeau 2013: np)

As we saw a little earlier, the big three medical model cognitive theories of autism have largely neglected the presence of autistic bodies. And yet, from as far back as Kanner's early descriptions of the young boys on whom his conceptualisation of autism was based, atypical sensory processing and motor responses have been part of the picture. Although still (for the most part) couched in a deficit perspective, research is finally beginning to take seriously the biologically based sensorimotor and perceptual differences associated with autism (see Proff *et al*, 2022 for review) and the ways in which they may cascade towards social differences and difficulties (and, indeed, we'll look at how they may be relevant to cross-neurotype communication breakdowns in Chapter 8).

Autistic people typically experience atypical – and often highly individual – patterns of hyper- or hypo-sensitivity to sensory stimuli. These differences can exist across all sensory domains, from the more familiar, external senses (sight, smell, touch, taste and hearing) to the less familiar internal senses (interoception – knowing your internal bodily states like hunger or when you need the toilet, proprioception – knowing where your body is in space and the vestibular sense – balance). We're not quite sure at the moment *why* autistic people have these sensory processing differences, but it's supposed that it's something like their sensory 'filters' (for each sensory modality) are set to different levels. For one sensory modality, they might take in lots of fine-meshed detail that others just wouldn't notice, and for others they might have the dial set at a higher setting so sensations aren't perceived or registered until the stimulus is really strong.

For many autistic people, the external sensory environments that have been designed for a mythically normal neurotypical 'can be extremely overwhelming and can present barriers for accessing certain places like supermarkets, eateries, large shops, schools and medical settings' (Manning *et al*, 2023). However, the sense of alienation can creep beyond the simply practical. In having a markedly divergent sensorily way of being in and experiencing the world, an autistic person's perceptual world can also 'turn out to be strikingly different from that of non-autistic people' (Bogdashina, 2016: 55):

> *'What if you're receiving the same sensory information as everyone else, but your brain is working differently? Then your experience of the world around you will be radically different from everyone else's, maybe even painfully so. In that case, you would literally be living in an alternate reality – an alternate sensory reality.'*
>
> (Grandin & Panek, 2014: 70).

With autistic and non-autistic people inhabiting sensory worlds (and *Umwelten*) that often differ dramatically from one another, is it any wonder that understanding one another often takes more work?

Monotropism

Possibly one of the most exciting and promising theories relating to autistic ways of being is the theory of *monotropism*, originally proposed by three autistic scholars, Dinah Murray, Mike Lesser and Wenn Lawson (2005). The monotropic account of autism addresses how autistic people process information cognitively. It begins from the position that the mind is, essentially, an interest system – it's constantly seeking out new information about the world around it to update its understanding – which is a similar starting place to that of the weak central coherence theory of autism and one that's largely agreed upon in the cognitive sciences (as we saw in Chapter 1).

The essential premise is that 'atypical strategies for the allocation of attention' (Murray *et al*, 2005: 139) are the central cause of numerous autistic social and behavioural characteristics. According to this account, the degree or breadth of attention allocation in humans is considered to be normally distributed and (largely) genetically determined, with some people possessing a greater tendency towards multiply focused attention (polytropism), and others a tendency towards more narrowly focused attention (monotropism). Autistic people will often find themselves at the far end of this distribution with a highly narrow 'attention tunnel'. Where non-autistic minds will comfortably entertain many simultaneous interests, each moderately aroused, the autistic mind will maintain only very few simultaneous interests, with each one highly aroused and intensely focused upon. It's a little bit like the difference between being in a dark room and having a very bright and intense torch light beaming on one small area, versus a less bright but wider-reaching lamp light softly illuminating a larger area. You'll see more things in the second case, but in less detail. Both can be useful.

The monotropic account, some argue, offers a unified explanation for the many different features associated with autism. The so-termed 'restricted and repetitive behaviours and interests' (see DSM-5 criteria, APA, 2013) can be explained by attention firing into 'monotropic superdrive' (Murray *et al*, 2005: 143) and entraining itself onto one self-pleasing task or topic. Social and communicative difficulties may come about as a consequence of a difficulty in processing, at speed, information from a variety of simultaneous channels (audio, visual, socio-cultural encyclopaedic knowledge, etc): a skill better suited to polytropic individuals with less narrowly and intensely focused attention. The atypical patterns of sensory experience (such as the hyper- and hypo-sensitivities to various sensory channels described above) might arise from some sensory inputs falling within the attention tunnel – and being processed, therefore, with heightened significance – and others falling outside, becoming virtually unnoticeable. In addition, monotropism can also explain what the predominant cognitive theories cannot, namely:

> '...*how individuals on the autism spectrum show a tendency toward either being passionately interested in a task or phenomena, or not interested at all, or how an unanticipated change 'within the attentional tunnel' can lead to a catastrophic disconnection from a previously 'safe' state of mind.*'
>
> (Milton, 2012a: 7)

As a possible theory of autism, the monotropic account is compelling. It also might explain the *heterogeneity* of autistic people; the focus of each autistic person's narrow tunnel of attention will vary considerably, creating highly idiosyncratic individuals. Despite this, monotropism has received little mainstream attention since its conception nearly 15 years ago. The fact that its proponents were autistic may have undermined its credibility as the value of autistic inclusion in autism research was yet to be enthusiastically embraced by the academy, despite a now growing movement towards participatory and insider research methodologies (that meaningfully include autistic people in research).

So there we have it. What *is* autism? I'm not sure we're much clearer, but at least we've covered the main ground of how people think and have thought about it over time. In the next chapter, we'll look more closely at the roles language and social communication have had to play in descriptions and understandings of autism before moving on, in Section 3, to look at cross-neurotype communication.

Chapter 5: Autistic language use: a short history

'Why wouldn't I be confused with language, people have their own meanings; people don't say what they mean and often they don't want to say what they mean...'
(Patricia Delmar, autistic woman, in Walsh et al, 2018: 117)

Communication has held a significant place in the definitions and descriptions of autism since its very beginnings. The observed, behavioural characteristics on which an autism diagnosis now hangs are rooted in Wing and Gould's (1979) 'Triad of Impairments', which include apparent 'impairments'[29] in communication as one of the three main areas of difference (along with seeming impairments in in social interaction and social imagination). Communication, in this context, refers to 'the full range of both verbal/linguistic and non-verbal (including gesture and intonation) means for interacting with others' (Tager-Flusberg, 1999: 325).

Numerous language and communication atypicalities have been associated with autism, and have come to shape its profile. So-called prototypical linguistic characteristics of autism include atypical prosody (i.e. an usual pattern of the intonation, stress and rhythm of speech), echolalia (i.e. the repetition of words and sounds out of context), and situational mutism (i.e. the temporary loss of your ability to use spoken words). However, it is 'pragmatic impairment' that is most consistently described and referred to across the diverse spectrum of autistic presentations, including age, gender and what was historically referred to in the literature as 'functioning-ability'[30] of individuals (Tager-Flusberg, 1996).

---

29 I'm using 'scare quotes' for the many times I have to write the word 'impairment' in this chapter – because, while it is a word that is very much part of the research and clinical literature about autistic language use, I personally find it distasteful and not quite correct.

30 One of the challenges of reporting on older research that used terms we no longer accept is that sometimes it's hard to know what to replace the terms with. Historically, high and low 'functioning ability' was sometimes used to describe the differences between different types of autism diagnoses (e.g. autism or Asperger's Syndrome), but sometimes was confused with whether autistic participants in studies had co-occurring learning disabilities. It's sometimes a stand-in for 'high or low support needs' – which is more accepted way of describing things these days – but this also remains complicated due to the fluctuating supports needs and abilities of individual autistic people dependent on changing circumstances and environment.

Pragmatics (see Chapter 3) is the area of linguistics most interested in language use (hence the title of this chapter) and meaning in context. For those with 'pragmatic impairment', we would expect them to have difficulty not so much with grammar and syntax or semantic meaning of words, but with the more social aspects of language. This includes things like a tendency toward literal interpretations of ambiguous or figurative language, an inability to identify when someone is joking or teasing, perseveration (getting 'stuck' on a topic loop), not knowing when to stop talking and making socially inappropriate comments. In other words, all things that require the use of theory of mind skills and intention recognition.

As we have seen in previous chapters, autistic people have long been cast as having significant 'impairments' in theory of mind abilities, to the extent that they have been described as 'mindblind' (Baron-Cohen, 1990). Yet some, including Dinishak and Akhtar (2013: 110), have argued that mindblindness as a metaphor 'obscures the fact that both [parties] contribute to the social and communicative difficulties between them'. In characterising the autistic person as mindblind, the natural reciprocity of social interaction is masked. It may also 'contribute to overlooking the ways in which autistic behaviours can be meaningful and/or adaptive' (*Ibid*).

In this chapter, we'll first take a look at the traditional view of autistic language use as 'impaired' that has shaped the diagnostic profile of autism. Following that, we'll delve into more recent, more neurodiversity-affirming ways of thinking about autistic communication and, finally, slide into the sonic world of spoken language as sensory pleasure.

The traditional view: autistic people as 'impaired' speakers

'Impairments' in the pragmatic use of language by autistic children were first documented in detail by Leo Kanner in 1943. Kanner noticed a striking commonality among a selection of the young boys under his care, in that they all seemed to experience difficulty in 'understanding that communication is about intended rather than literal or surface meaning [and] failure to view conversations as a means of modifying and extending the cognitive environment of a conversational partner' (Tager-Flusberg, 1999: 331).

Idiosyncratic language use

Taken as the most common indicator of a poor grasp of the pragmatic uses of language was the idiosyncratic use of words and phrases. If a speaker is using words and expressions that others cannot be expected to understand, they are hardly acting as a *helpful speaker* (see Chapter 3). Because we can usually safely assume that speakers wish to be understood, the use of unhelpful or unintelligible words or phrases has been taken as a sign that these speakers don't understand what their audience does and does not know. In the example of young Paul G, one of Kanner's case studies, he would frequently offer up utterances that – to Kanner – seemed nonsensical, such as 'Don't throw the dog off the balcony', 'The people in the hotel', 'Did you hurt your leg?', and 'Peten-eater' (Kanner, 1943: 227). According to Kanner:

> *'None of these remarks was meant to have communicative value. There was, on his side, no affective tie to people. He behaved as if people as such did not matter or even exist.'*
> (Kanner, 1943: 228)

Yet the assertion that these utterances carried no communicative intent is probably far too bold and belies the dehumanising undertones of the pathology paradigm that Kanner was working within. For instance, in the case of the last, rather unusual phrase ('Peten-eater!'), Paul G's mother thought it was traceable back to a moment when she had dropped a saucepan loudly on the kitchen floor while reciting the 'Peter, Peter, pumpkin-eater' nursery rhyme to him. There is clearly some shared, affective experience that is being referred to by the repetition of this phrase, however ineffective it might seem at first glance to an impartial observer who does not share the reference.

A similar example can be found in the case of JS, a three-year-old autistic boy also under Kanner's purview. Whenever he was asked if he was being honest, he would respond with the nonsense word, 'Blum!' This peculiarity was eventually explained when JS (who could already read fluently) was able to point to an advertisement proclaiming 'Blum tells the Truth!' (Happé, 1991: 214). Both Kanner and, later, Happé (a significant shaper of autism discourse) read this as an example of the autistic boy expressing a private (and therefore ineffectual) association, as opposed to a culturally shared one (such as 'Romeo' standing in for 'all lovers', *Ibid*). In using his own private associations without apparent thought to whether these could be understood by others, JS was interpreted as not being able to know (or put into action the knowledge that) other people have different minds and don't always know what he knows. This analysis, however, seems to me to overlook the brightness of a fluently, independently reading three-year-old and the fact that such a child might, on encountering a public text in the public domain, assume that its associations and referents are culturally shared. From within the medical model, quick to measure against a mythical norm, such creative idiosyncrasies soon became examples of impairments that, ultimately, were rubber-stamped as diagnostic criteria.

Taking things literally

One common stereotype in representations of autistic people is the tendency towards 'extreme literalness' (Bogdashina, 2005: 181). This, too, has roots in Kanner's early observations. Donald T was Kanner's first autistic case study, who seemed to lean towards literal interpretations of utterances (their evident semantic meaning) above interpretations that required any degree of inferencing. Kanner (1943: 220), for example, described Donald T as responding to the request to 'Put that down' by putting whatever he was holding on the floor (rather than, as Kanner had intended, for him to simply 'let go' of whatever he was holding).

Happé also shared a similar observation from her work with autistic children:

> 'Interacting with a bright and verbal autistic child can be an eye-opening experience: One discovers one is talking in metaphors! A request to "Stick your coat down over there" is met by a serious request for glue. Ask if she will "give you a hand," and she will answer that she needs to keep both hands and cannot cut one off to give you...'
>
> (Happé, 1995: 275)

As well as these kinds of difficulties with idiomatic language (i.e. colloquial, figurative language such as 'stop beating around the bush'), an extension of an extreme literalness is often the missing of irony, sarcasm or metaphor: features of language that require a multifaceted interpretation and theory of mind perspective-taking skills. However, while a tendency towards literal interpretations over pragmatically enriched inferences has formed a key part of the linguistic profile of autism, it may not be as fundamental as was originally thought.

Two studies (Chevallier *et al*, 2010, and Pijnacker *et al*, 2009), for example, both found that their autistic participants were just as able to produce *scalar inferences* as the non-autistic participants. As with all pragmatic inferences, 'scalar inferences' require the hearer 'to go beyond the linguistic meaning in order to recognise what the speaker intended to convey' (Chevallier *et al*, 2010: 3). Specifically, 'the core idea is that the choice of a weaker element from a scale ... tends to implicate that, as far as the speaker knows, none of the stronger elements in the scale holds in this instance' (Carston, 1998: 179). For example, the following scalar inferences (b) can be drawn from the following utterances (a):

1. (a) Some of those bees by the hive entrance are drones.

   (b) i.e. *Not **all** of the bees by the entrance are drones.*

2. (a) There are 24 species of bumblebee in the UK.

   (b) i.e. *There aren't **more** than 24 species of bumblebee in the UK.*

In Chevallier *et al*'s (2010) study, 22 adolescent autistic males and 22 non-autistic matched control participants were shown a series of straightforward images while an audio-recorded statement describing the images was played to them. They were tasked simply with saying whether the statement was true or false in relation to the image before them. Each statement contained a connective ('AND' or 'OR') and in some cases the 'OR' was contrastively stressed when it was spoken (i.e. 'there is a horse OR a goat', Chevallier *et al*, 2010: 12). Logically, in the 'OR' condition, the utterance may be interpreted to mean 'there is a horse, or a goat, or a horse and a goat'. However, when contrastive stress is applied to the 'OR', hearers should be oriented towards an inferentially enriched interpretation ('there is a horse OR a goat: but not both'). In such cases, when shown an image of both a horse AND a goat, participants making scalar inferences should say that the statement is false. To the surprise of the authors, the autistic group performed at the same level as the non-autistic control group. These findings replicated those of an unrelated but contemporaneous study by Pijnacker *et al* (2009) which investigated the phenomenon of scalar inferencing among autistic adults. Together, they challenged the then-prevailing narrative that autistic people universally experience pragmatic impairment.

Atypical prosody

In addition to the issues with pragmatic uses of language outlined above, autistic use of prosody has also long been flagged as (pathologically) atypical, or as somehow 'unusual or odd-sounding' (McCann & Peppé, 2003). *Prosody* refers to the pattern of intonation (the kind of musicality of speech) that lays over a full utterance (i.e. it is 'suprasegmental') rather than just a one word or phrase, and involves things like tone, volume and rhythm. The type of atypical prosody perhaps most commonly associated with autistic speech is one that is 'monotonous' and flat (Hubbard *et al*, 2017 – i.e. having less variation in tone and rhythm). However, they are also often described as having intonation that is *too* colourful (i.e. with an unusually wide range of pitch and tone that is sometimes described as 'sing-song' (McCann & Peppé, 2003)). Sometimes autistic speaking speed is noticeably faster or slower than that of (mythically normal) neurotypical people; sometimes it's noticeably louder, sometimes noticeably quieter, and sometimes autistic people appear to have an adopted accent different from that of their peers (*Ibid*).

Occasionally referred to as *dysprosody* (Stribling *et al*, 2006), this apparent failure to correctly produce (neuro)typical prosodic features has often been interpreted as an indication of an autistic person's 'lack of access to the meaning inferred by prosodic variation in talk' (*Ibid*). Prosody is an essential factor for successful communication; 'the way we say the words we say helps us convey the meanings we intend' (Wharton, 2012: 567). Modulation of volume, length and pitch of syllables and sentences 'help direct a listener's attention to the most salient points of a message' (*Ibid*). We can use tone to express affect (i.e. feeling of mood) or to indicate our position in relation to the propositions we are expressing (e.g. irony, mocking, incredulity, etc). An inability to correctly employ or interpret prosody could lead to serious difficulties in accessing the pragmatic content of an utterance.

In one more recent study, Hubbard and colleagues (2017) set out to examine the affective, rather than the pragmatic or grammatical, prosody of autistic adults. Recordings were made of 15 (notably, all male) autistic adults with a mean age of 21 years, saying aloud a set of five emotionally ambiguous phrases (e.g., 'I can't believe this'), in five emotional contexts: neutral, happy, interested, sad and angry. In order to elicit the relevant affective content, before each recording, participants were asked to recall a moment in their recent personal history where they had felt that emotion. The recordings were then played to 52 listeners (of whom 22 were autistic) who were drawn from a pool of undergraduates from the School of Behavioral and Brain Sciences at the University of Texas at Dallas. These listeners were asked to (a) identify the emotion expressed and (b) rate its 'level of naturalness' (Hubbard *et al*, 2017: 1991).

The results add to our knowledge of prosody in autism in an interesting way. In terms of the production of prosodic features, in comparison to the control (non-autistic) group, the autistic speakers 'produced phrases with greater intensity, longer durations, and increased pitch range for all emotions except neutral' (*Ibid*). In other words, they demonstrated autistically typical, atypical prosody. From this, the researchers concluded that a heightened intensity of prosodic features may be related to specific emotional contexts. Both non-autistic and autistic listeners were better able to identify the emotions expressed by the autistic group of speakers (compared to the non-autistic speakers), but went on to rate them as sounding less natural. In summary, what this study indicates is that autistic speakers *are* able to use prosody effectively to both convey and read emotional states, but that the increased variability in pitch, velocity, and greater length of utterances marks their speech out as sounding somehow 'less natural'[31].

This fits with a growing pattern of research that demonstrates the frequency with which non-autistic people tend to form negative, thin-slice judgements (or negative 'first impressions') about autistic people (see Chapter 6 for more on that). While a really enlightening study, what it says, exactly, about autistic prosody remains a little unclear. On the one hand, the raters in the study were all undergraduate students at a university which, at the time, had the highest number of autistic student enrolments in the USA (Morrison *et al*, 2019a). It may be that by virtue of having greater exposure to autistic peers, non-autistic raters were more familiar with autistic modes of expression than, say, the wider public might be. This may have influenced the ease with which they seemed to be able to interpret the autistic speaker's atypical prosody. On another

---

31 Rather than less 'natural', perhaps it is as simple as it being less common.

hand, while researchers noticed the link between atypical prosody and specific emotions, we don't have enough information yet to understand why that might be. The fact that autistic and non-autistic speakers express affect differently (through prosody) may be a linguistic issue, but it may also reflect an integral difference in the experiencing of the emotions. As we saw in the last chapter, autistic people often experience hyper- or hyposensitivity to sensory stimuli across all domains: including interoception, which includes the sensing of feeling states. It is plausible that for some autistic participants to register an emotion as significant enough to warrant expressing – and, if you recall, they were asked to draw on recent personal memories of having experienced the target emotion – the feeling would already need to be intense.

New turn: the intersubjectivity framework

Over the last two decades, social science research into autistic sociality and communication has begun to turn its gaze towards intersubjectivity. *Intersubjectivity* is the phenomenological position that, as collaborative, cognising beings, humans live beyond the bounds of our corporeal and perceptual fields and, at an embodied level, are consciously engaged with each other (see Gillespie, 2011). It is the view that as embodied, social agents, we share in some degree of a 'co-conception or co-orientation to the world' (Schegloff, 1992: 1296). Rather than focusing on individual functioning, intersubjectivity approaches emphasise the inter-relational aspects of selves. In that sense, they potentially align well with the neurodiversity paradigm that takes an *ecological view* of neuro-minority disablement (i.e. one that takes into account the roles of the physical, cultural and social environments in disabling neurodivergent people).

In linguistic anthropology

A special issue of *Ethos*, the journal of the Society for Psychological Anthropology, was published in 2010 entitled 'Autism: rethinking the possibilities'. Anthropology – and linguistic anthropology – are fields of research essentially focused on human society and cultures, and in the latter case, how language is used in those contexts. In this special edition, a collection of papers was featured that 'reimagine[d] autism from a phenomenological, rather than a biomedical, point of view' (Solomon & Bagatell, 2010: 2), embracing the diversity of autism and placing the personal experience of those who live with it (i.e. the broader familial and support networks as well as the autistic individuals themselves) at the centre of the research. In the field of autistic language use research, this was pretty radical.

Many of the papers offer sensitive analyses of large bodies of transcribed conversational data featuring autistic children: ultimately presenting them as situated, interactive agents within their familiar worlds (Sirota, 2010) and as demonstrating a unique kind of 'autistic sociality' (Ochs & Solomon, 2010 – more on this in Chapter 6).

Most relevant here is a paper by Sterponi and Fasulo (2010). Through a case study analysis of one autistic child (aged five years and ten months) in dialogue with his caregivers, their observation was that autism might be thought of as signifying the 'boundaries of what we regard as human sociability and communication' (Sterponi & Fasulo, 2010: 117). The researchers argued that the commonly accepted binary distinction between, at the one end, functional, normative communicative ability and, at the other, deficiency or impairment:

> '...fails to recognize that mundane communicative interaction is punctuated by departures from normativity and that those departures not only do not break down communication but also are often the measure of felicitous interpersonal exchanges.'
> (Sterponi & Fasulo, 2010: 117)

(Mythically) 'normal' communicative performance is not, they argue, such a stable a construct as we might perhaps require it to be if it is to be used as a benchmark against which 'impairments' are to be measured. With this in mind, Sterponi and Fasulo (2010) sought to investigate the atypical language use of this autistic child (pseudonymised as 'Aaron'), beginning with the premise of asking 'what is this utterance doing?' instead of automatically problematising it.

As their data, the researchers analysed 16 hours of video footage recorded over the duration of one month, documenting spontaneous talk-in-interaction (i.e. everyday chit-chat). In their analysis, Sterponi and Fasulo rely heavily on the concept of *progressivity*, drawing on Schegloff's

(1992) development of the conversation analytic[32] notion of common knowledge as procedurally generated. For Schegloff, the puzzle of how intersubjectivity could be achieved in interaction seemed best explained by the scaffolding of 'a set of practices by which actions and stances could be composed in a fashion which displayed grounding in, and orientation to, "knowledge held in common"' (1992: 1298). Mutual understanding could thus be seen – rather than being based on seemingly inexplicable and nebulous 'commonsense knowledge' (*Ibid*) – as to be in a constant process of co-creation between interlocutors, driven by sequential turn-taking. 'Progressivity', which Sterponi and Fasulo describe as the ability for interlocutors to *go on with one another*, is contingent on this procedural intersubjectivity:

> *'The procedural infrastructure of interaction offers a host of resources that interlocutors routinely employ to display and evaluate understanding. In other words, talk in interaction is organized in such a way that from the way turns are tied to one another, interlocutors can implicitly and continuously assess their reciprocal alignment, and go on with next move if they detect no (or no significant) mismatch. Progressivity, namely the unfolding of the interaction, is thus ensured by its own functioning.'*
> (Sterponi and Fasulo, 2010: 119)

Focusing their attention this way on progressivity within the transcribed conversations revealed some communicative competencies on the part of Aaron that would likely previously have been missed. Where Aaron seemed to lack some of the functional communicative resources common to neurotypical children of his age (such as protests, assessments, narrations, etc.), he was nevertheless able to apply the communicative moves he had mastery over in such a way as to 'propel sequence progressivity' (Sterponi & Fasulo, 2010: 120).

In several instances, for example, when faced with a parental request for a specific behaviour or response, Aaron would reply with the phrase 'or else?' Because Aaron had limited lexical range, this phrase became something of a common move and, under a less generous analysis, might have been interpreted as a rote response or what is often referred

---

[32] Conversation analysis is a methodology in linguistics research that is interested in seeing how mutual understanding is achieved in verbal communication.

to in the autism literature as 'stereotypy' (i.e. a seemingly purposeless repetition of an act). It was, in fact, rather a clever move. As the authors noted, it neither directly refused nor complied with the request, but 'shifts discourse to a hypothetical plane... suspending the behavioural demands and launching a new language game' (Sterponi & Fasulo, 2010: 124). It functions, here, in a similar way as Bartleby the Scrivener's 'I would prefer not to' (Melville, 1961). In these interactions, Aaron gains control and incites his parents to keep the conversation running (rather than, say, end at the fulfilled directive).

What is most interesting about the above case study are the excerpts shared where progressivity extends over lengthy conversations, held together by linguistic playfulness. In one, where Aaron and his mum sit on his bed and joke about a bug that has entered the room, 'language is set free and allowed to run along the very edges of meaning' (Sterponi & Fasulo, 2010: 135). Conversational turns take a sensorial, phatic (i.e. expressing sociability rather than specific meaning) lead rather than a semantic one: in the sense that word repetitions, alliterations (i.e. sound repetitions) and prosodic parallelisms (e.g. rhythm and tone-matching) drive each next utterance:

226 MOM	That's the bug blanket
227 AARON	*(laughs, turns to reach bedside)* bug
228 MOM	It's [the bug blanket
229 AARON	[bug- (.) bug hug *((getting on bed))*
230 MOM	Bug hug
231 AARON	*((laughs))*
232 MOM	Bug hug (.) bat bath
233 AARON	Wo no bath
234 MOM	Tap rap
235 AARON	No [bath
236 MOM	[(tub)
237 AARON	No bath
238 MOM	Yes bath
239 AARON	Or else? *((laughing))*

240 MOM   Or else?

241 AARON Stink *((laughs))*

(Sterponi & Fasulo, 2010: 134-135)[33]

The sequence culminates in 'pure speech and sound play, a vocal, rhythmical duet of consonant variation' around the word 'bug' (Sterponi & Fasulo, 2010: 134). Like two jazz musicians improvising together, a tight, intersubjective attunement is evident between Aaron and his mother as the conversation continues. In this and similar moments, what makes them work is that Aaron's interlocutors allow their grip on expected responses to loosen, and take the leap of faith required to take his moves as they come, trusting in Aaron's capacity to participate in the exchange on his own terms.

Echolalia

Sterponi builds upon this curiosity-driven methodological approach in later research papers investigating autistic language use, including in one with de Kirby (2016). In this, they analyse a small corpus of spontaneously occurring conversational data featuring three six-year-old autistic children and members of their immediate family. As with her earlier work, they found that some of the key characteristics that might traditionally be described as 'impaired' autistic language use – such as pragmatically atypical utterances, echolalia and pronoun atypicality – seemed to have potentially alternative explanations.

For example, instances of echolalia under this nuanced analysis were often revealed to involve a discrete functional purpose; in one case it served as a distraction tactic to divert a parent interlocutor from a conversational direction that the child did not wish to engage with. In their transcribed conversations they also saw that echolalia was functioning, at times as a 'mechanism to experience the other, or to access the experience of the other' (Sterponi & de Kirby, 2016: 402), or in other words, it could be interpreted as a divergent form of perspective-taking.

In a review of language and speech studies in autism, Gernsbacher *et al* (2016), who remind us that echolalia is common to all children during their language development, argue that it *can* have 'communicative' (2016:

---

33 The unusual punctuation in this extract reflects the transcription conventions used to capture things like overlapping speech (e.g. square brackets) and to show the transcribers' descriptions (e.g. in double brackets). A full list of transcription conventions can be found in Appendix 2.

417) and 'generative' (2016: 418) functions. They demonstrate this in the case of Bud, a young autistic boy:

> 'For example, Bud, an autistic child who was quite fond of the Teletubbies television show, initially echoed the sentence, "One day in Teletubbyland, all of the Teletubbies were very busy when suddenly a big rain cloud appeared." Weeks later, using mitigated echolalia, the child said, "One day in Bud's house, Mama and Bud were very busy when suddenly Daddy appeared," to express the construct of his father returning home.'
>
> (Gernsbacher *et al*, 2016, 417- 418)

While Bud was not yet at the linguistic stage where he was able to generate novel two-word phrases, he nonetheless adapted a complex echolalic sentence to express his feelings about his father coming home.

Hanne De Jaegher (2013) offers one further angle on the function of echolalia in an autistic child's speech in a paper outlining her enactive account of autism and 'sense-making' (more on this in Chapter 7). She first recounts an interaction involving echolalia reported on in a study undertaken by Stribling *et al* (2006). The original authors had analysed three cases where their autistic child participant, 'Lenny', inserts what they call 'spelling assertions' (Stribing *et al*, 2006: 9, 14) – e.g. 'please has got an A in it' – into a context where spelling appeared irrelevant. Taking into account the interactional context (Lenny was playing with a robot at the time but his spelling assertions were issued at times when someone else was in control of it) and the prosodic features (these utterances were delivered at a yelling pitch that diverged from the surrounding contributions and mirrored protest intonation), the authors had concluded that these spelling assertions were functioning as protests against losing control of the toy, and an attempt to regain it. In her complementary analysis, De Jaegher wonders whether the echolalia may also bear an alternative, intrinsic function:

> 'From the enactive point of view, in which a cognizer self-maintains and self-organizes, it can be proposed that the boy is self-affirming his place in an interaction in which he feels that something is taken away from him, by uttering knowledge that he has. These

> *utterances could be a way of maintaining individual autonomy in an interactional situation.'*
>
> (De Jaegher, 2013: 13)

Furthermore, as Lenny's spelling assertions seemed to follow prompts from what the robot itself had said (e.g. immediately prior to Lenny uttering *'please has got an A in it'*, the robot had uttered the word *'please'*) it may be that Lenny was *going on with* the robot in his own unique way.

Atypical pronoun use

One additional and commonly reported atypical use of language by autistic people – and in particular by autistic children – is the phenomenon of pronoun reversals (Naigles *et al*, 2016). This involves switching first-person pronouns ('I') for second-person ('you'), or third ('him', 'her' or the child's own name). For example, a child might say 'you want some more juice' when what they mean is '*I* want some more juice', or 'give Gemma some more gravy, please' instead of 'give *me* some more gravy, please'[34].

As with echolalia, Gernsbacher *et al* (2016: 416) outline in their review how atypical pronoun use is not unique to autism and that where it does occur, any significant differences between autistic and non-autistic difficulties are dissolved when careful matching of the children's language comprehension skills in undertaken. They highlight how, by virtue of the original lens under which autism was identified and scrutinised being a psychoanalytic one, a bias was established to label characteristics immediately as deficits.

Sterponi and de Kirby (2016) found similarly alternative interpretations for the reversals of first- and third-person pronouns by some autistic children. When examined in the broader communicative contexts, these reversals often seemed to reflect an adoption of the 'babytalk' framework initiated by the autistic child's interlocutor (e.g. parent or caregiver). Babytalk, with its 'heightened pitch, exaggerated intonation, stretched out sounds, reduplications, endearments and infantilising lexicon' (Ochs, 2012: 152) is the kind of cooing mode of speaking adults often use with young infants. It is auditorily soothing, and as such has the potential to 'immerse interlocutors in an affective zone of intense intimacy' (*Ibid*)[35]. In Sterponi

---

[34] Gemma can never get enough gravy.
[35] However, as Ochs and Solomon (2010: 85) observe, the 'heightened affect and slowed tempo' may prove unwittingly distracting for autistic children.

and de Kirby's (2016) analysis, they found that adult interlocutors often began the babytalk framework – which included them referring to themselves in the third person (e.g. 'give mummy a cuddle...' rather than 'give me a cuddle'). In the instances where autistic children were reversing their own pronouns, this often seemed to be a continuation of the babytalk framework rather than – as has typically been assumed, based on the theory of mind deficit view of autism – a fundamental confusion of self and other.

Language as sensory experience

I'm sitting in a GP surgery consulting room, late summer, in a derelict seaside town. The air conditioning whirs persistently from beyond the articulated beige leather couch and the roll of blue paper towel mounted on the wall beside it. Behind me, a stainless steel trolley of phlebotomy equipment insists that the knees of my crossed legs bump up against the desk I'm sitting beside. The back of my neck is cold.

We're going for 'the jackpot'.

We have 20 minutes left of today's Cognitive Behavioural Therapy session — I'm here to try and get myself through this PhD mess, to not lose my grip of it, my grip of myself — and out comes a new, over-photocopied form. We hurry through to the third column: the one where you write down-

'evidence you have for your core belief'.

My therapist is from the Baltic states and says the word 'belief' with a 'dark L' (/ɫ/). He lands heavily on the 'L', sounding it out the way you would pronounce the 'L' at the end of 'full'. I like it. It loops round in my mind on repeat,

BuLLLief — BuLLLLLief — BuLLLLief

BuLLLief — BuLLLLLief — BuLLLLief

BuLLLief -

***

From as far back as Kanner's (1943) early case studies, an autistic delight in the sound of words, as opposed to their meaning, has been noted. Echolalic repetitions and perseverations pepper the sometimes-limited speech of the autistic children under observation, as was described in the case of Donald T:

> 'He seemed to have much pleasure in ejaculating words or phrases, such as "Chrysanthemum"; "dahlia, dahlia, dahlia"; "Business"; "Trumpet vine"...'[36]
>
> (Kanner, 1943: 219)

For any autistic readers, I'm sure many of you will recognise the repetitious joy of sounding out a favourite new word or an ear-worm jingle or phrase. And one additional, common thread that runs through these more phenomenologically grounded approaches to autistic language use is the acknowledgement of an – at times – increased attunement to the sensorial aspects of words and phrases.

In a recent commentary, Sterponi (2018) observed the following:

> 'Autistic engagement with language is often experientially attuned to sound and form, in excess of semantic content, thereby revealing of dimensions of significance that tend to be overlooked in autism research... Conjuring up realities through referential operations is undoubtedly a chief semiotic capacity of language. There is also semiotic potential, however, in the musicality of phrases and their articulatory texture—as they are experienced in ear and in mouth. Autistic modes of engagement with language subvert the referential hegemony to uncover additional dimensions of significance and experience of language.'
>
> (Sterponi, 2018: 177)

Words and phrases clearly possess a sensory dimension, yet it is rare amid the flux of everyday conversation that most speakers stop to pay

---

36 *Chrysanthemum; dahlia, dahlia, dahlia; business; trumpet vine!* Trumpet vine! Say those words aloud. Elongate them. Shout them if you dare! Roll the 'R's. It's impossible not to feel like the tongue is breaking the greatest taboo: speaking nonsense words for the sheer alchemical pleasure of sound and articulation combined. In the right circumstances, it may even verge on the ecstatic...

attention to the way their mouth feels when they sound out a word, to the resonance it generates in their chest, or back, or throat or the way it tickles the ear. Semantic meanings and inference interpretations dominate limited processing capacities. A simple delighting in the rhythm and music of language is left, in most cases, for the realm of poetry or song.

This recognition of a heightened autistic engagement with the sensorial element of language seems to accord with a *gestalt*[37] perception that may be typical of autistic people (i.e. where whole sensory scenes are perceived as single entities with seemingly insignificant sensory percepts not filtered out (see Bogdashina, 2005, and Walker, 2019)). Echolalia that doesn't have an obvious communicative function may fall into this category: as 'auditory-tactile/sensory-linguistic toys' (Bogdashina, 2005: 177) that may be repeated as a source of self-soothing or self-enjoyment, in a not wholly dissimilar manner to meditation mantras. In fact, a growing number of neurodiversity-affirming speech and language therapists who work with the idea of *gestalt language processing* – a mode of language acquisition seen to be built around learning chunked meaning phrases first, before individual words (Prizant, 1982) – with autistic children and families under their care describe echolalia as part of this language-learning process.

Linguistic anthropologist Eleanor Ochs argues for an increased consideration of the additional qualities of language beyond that which receives the most attention: the symbolic. The symbolic dimension of language relates to its capacity to represent facts of the objective world along with 'public cultural meanings' while bearing no necessary 'resemblance to the represented' (Ochs, 2012: 142). Language can be indexical (i.e. pointing to things in the world) and performative (e.g. performing functions such as promising or declaring). For Ochs, however, language use can also be a (phenomenological) *mode of experiencing*.

As a demonstration of her argument, Ochs provides the transcript of an interaction between 'Adam', an 11-year-old autistic boy, and his mother in which Adam recounts 'with great relish' (2012: 150) and in great detail the exact times that the school bell rings throughout the day. In their conversation, Adam speaks enthusiastically about what he considers to be the 'craziness' of the bell times (e.g. at 08:31 or 09:28), whipping up his mother into his excitement with punctuating claps and laughter. Under Ochs' analysis, the emphatic delivery – it is annotated in the transcripts

---

37 'Gestalt' is German for 'unified whole'.

as being breathy, full of affect and highly marked by tonal stress – and repetitiveness 'transports him and his mother inside the temporal domain of Mrs Brown's first-period class' (Ochs, 2012: 151). As well as its ability to conjure a reality, there is an evident pleasure in the use of language itself, in a manner reminiscent of autistic 'stimming':

> 'Like rocking back-and-forth and spinning, the voiced repetitions, sequences, and contrasts of the class times are co-experienced as emergent sources of pleasure and shared laughter.'
>
> (Ochs, 2012: 151)

This view of language as a *mode of experiencing* is exemplified in the extreme in a pioneering video essay called 'In My Language' (2007: see Appendix 1). In it, non-speaking autistic activist Meg Baggs first gives viewers a glimpse of their 'native language' and then, in the second half, introduces a 'translation' via a text-to-speech synthesiser with closed captions layered over the top of the visuals. In the video, to demonstrate their language, Baggs 'films themselves rhythmically stroking the clicking-keys on a computer keyboard, flapping their fingers before the camera lens while droning vocal tones, rattling looped coat-hanger wire around a metal door handle, and rocking back and forwards while sniffing a book' (Heasman *et al*, in prep: np.). When the audio comes in, Baggs explains:

> '...my language is not about designing words or even visual symbols for people to interpret. It is about being in a constant conversation with every aspect of my environment. Reacting physically to all parts of my surroundings [...] I smell things. I listen to things. I feel things. I taste things. I look at things...'
>
> (Baggs, 2007)

Outside the realm of autism studies, some of these observations relating to the role of the sonic dimension of language have been drawn out by Kugler (2002), based on Jung's early work on word association. In the early 20th century, Jung worked at the Burghölzli Klinik in Zürich, under the supervision of Eugen Bleuler.[38] One of Jung's main research tasks was

---

[38] Coincidentally, it was during his work in the Burghölzli Klinik that Bleuler coined the term 'autism'.

to test some of Freud's theories of the origins of psychopathology and in order to do this he conducted a number of experiments that often involved word association tests, administered to participants who were under states of increasing amounts of induced fatigue. In addition to the findings tied to the original research aims, Jung also noticed some unusual phenomena. As fatigue increased, a participant's semantic (meaning) associations would reduce and be replaced by phonetic word associations:

> 'The more tired the subject became, the less his associations were influenced by the meaning of the stimulus word and the more the subject tended to associate words according to a similarity in sound.'
> (Kugler, 2002: 26)

In a battery of two-hundred word associations, they found that after the first hundred, participants would become bored, pay less attention and demonstrate a significant decrease in the semantic associations made alongside an increase in the phonetic ones. A similar tendency towards phonetic associations was seen in those participants who were tested immediately after waking from some physically restorative sleep, yet who remained cognitively drowsy. From this, the researchers concluded that, as attention and cognitive resources decrease, so too does the inhibition of what they thought to be the first order subconscious associations: the phonetic ones.

This knowledge may help us move a little closer to understanding why it is that, in autistic language use, the sensorial, phonetic attributes of words can carry seemingly heightened salience. The Burghölzli Klinik research suggested that the centrally salient content of the mental representations of words are its phonetic components; it is these that are most deeply embedded in our subconscious. Increased cognitive effort, in the form of attention, is required to process the next layer of semantic associations. This is purely speculation, but it's possible that autistic individuals, with their divergent, often monotropic attentional patterns, have sufficient intensity of attention directed elsewhere (*deep tunnelling thoughts about honeybees, scratchy background noise, a weird feeling in my toe, oh! a birdy!*) so as to not be directed away from the *sound* of the words by the *meaning*-content…

...bug / hug / bed / bug / bite / bit / bug bite / bug blanket / bad bed...

In this section, we have taken a whistle-stop tour through the different ways in which autism has been described from its early conception up to the present day, and looked a little at autistic language use and communication. In the following section, we'll tackle the issue at the heart of this book: why does cross-neurotype communication often not seem to work very well, and how might we do better at it?

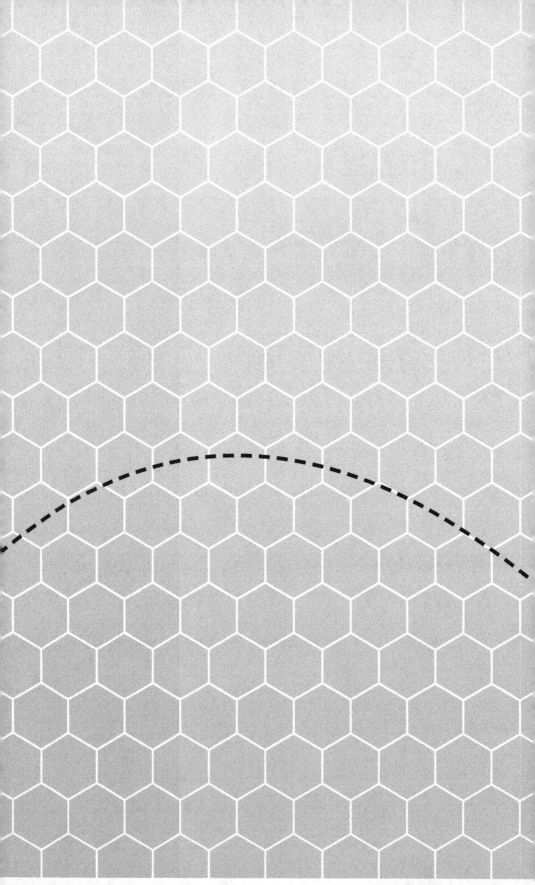

Section 3
It takes two: Sharing meaning with an 'Other'

Chapter 6: The double empathy problem

Out back, the pub garden was spiced with plums and crab apples, dipping their branches low. Lingering evening sun dappled the faces of the few other wedding guests who had also come outside to finish their meal, perched like bright birds around one, large, circular table.

The cackling, giggling, prosecco-sipping mass waved a few arms out towards me as I stepped down onto the cobbled path.

"Come sit with us, sweetheart! We can make room!"

To the left of them, on the other side of the path in a shady area was one slightly older, solitary, grey-suited man. Feet planted squarely on the floor, knees bent at right angles, hands folded neatly into his lap. Dark blue socks, dark blue bow tie.

Calling back my thanks, I picked my way, slowly, over to the shaded side, cautious not to spill my fizz as I moved, dodging a hefty bumble bee as she thrummed past my head.

'Do you mind if I join you?' I asked, my voice soft, eyes down to the ground.

'Oh no, no! No, please, no, please sit down!'

As I ate my dessert, slowly savouring each mouthful, I tentatively offered some to Martha's older brother: the brother I'd somehow not really clocked Martha had in these past 15 years until, on receiving my invite to the wedding, and when I'd reminded her I'm not always great in crowds and that I might need to take myself away at some point, she'd reassured me her brother was similarly prone to social anxiety and overwhelm, and likely wouldn't feel like talking much to anyone.

Martha's brother took up my offer of some brownie and reciprocated with a fresh raspberry from his Eton Mess. We continued to sit in silence together, occasionally nodding and smiling for five minutes, for ten minutes... I liked his quiet company. After hours of small talk and catching up with old friends, and pleases and thankyous and oh my goodness your child has growns! this sitting together was a solace. Easy.

Mmm! Martha's brother would occasionally murmur, spooning meringue into his mouth.

Mmm! I'd agree, rolling chocolate around my tongue.

As we both stared ahead, resting our eyes on the grass blades quivering in the breeze, a small bird alighted on the ground before us.

'What, what, what kind of bird do you think that is then?' Martha's brother asked me and — VOILA! — birds had once been a special interest of mine, so I tumbled into a rusty repertoire of animated facts and anecdotes, with Martha's brother chuckling now. He made a joke about Doctor Who, something I didn't fully understand because I hadn't gotten around to watching any Doctor Who before (something I've since remedied), but what I did understand was the gist of the joke so I found myself laughing with him, and it felt funny! And I told him I didn't really know much about Doctor Who as I didn't have a television and lived on a boat, which he found funny! And we spoke about my boat, and his room where he lived in his mum's house, and what we liked to do in our spaces and...

From nowhere, Martha was standing in front of us, beautiful, backlit by the low sun in her vintage dress, announcing the arrival of the taxi that had come to take Martha's brother home. We'd been sat there for the best part of an hour...

***

One of the greatest challenges for autistic people is difficulty with social communication. For many, the frequent, micro (and macro) misunderstandings and the resultant ruptures to rapport and interpersonal attunement create a pervasive sense of, at best, not fitting in and, at worse, profound loneliness and alienation (Quadt, Williams *et al*, 2023). Breakdowns in mutual understanding don't only impact personal relationships but create barriers to accessing vital healthcare (Doherty *et al*, 2022), education and employment (see Chapter 10), chronically affecting the person's quality of life. Historically, as we've seen in earlier chapters, the medical model has framed these troubles with social communication as arising from inherent autistic impairments: in particular from assumedly impoverished theory of mind abilities. However, as we've also seen, the stereotype that autistic people uniquely struggle with theory of mind skills is gradually being dismantled. In the past 12 years, an alternative theory, proposed by an autistic scholar and emanating from a difference-not-deficit, social model of disability framework, has begun to gain momentum both in research efforts and wider public awareness. That theory? The *double empathy problem*.

The double empathy problem: what is it?

In 2012, autistic sociologist Damian Milton crystallised an idea he had been working with for some time. Rather than autistic people simply not being very good at social communication or understanding how other people feel – the narrative thus far presented by medical model autism theorists – it might instead be that the significant differences in the lived experience of autistic and non-autistic people mean that it is harder work to understand one another and, crucially, that this runs in both directions.

According to Milton, cross-neurotype communication (i.e. between two speakers of different neurotypes) is best thought of as being troubled by 'a disjuncture in reciprocity between two differently disposed social actors' (Milton, 2012: 884) who 'hold different norms and expectations of each other' (Milton *et al*, 2018: 1). In other words, interpersonal attunement is harder in these circumstances because autistic and non-autistic people have very different *dispositions* (with less experiential common ground). Because social communication is intersubjective and interactions are scaffolded as they develop, social subtext is something that is actively constructed by those involved. With markedly different *ways of being* in the world, the chance for misunderstanding between neurotypes is high.

For autistic people, there is a 'pertinent personal requirement' to understand – or make the extra efforts to try to understand – the other minds of non-autistic people in order to 'survive and potentially thrive in a non-[autistic] culture' (Milton, 2012: 886). Living in a neurotypically-designed and neurotypically-dominant world, it is essential for autistic people to sensitise themselves to neurotypical *ways of being* and to develop ways of traversing the gap between dispositions. For non-autistic people, there is no such imperative. As such, and simply by virtue of the fact that autistic people meet far more neurotypical people than neurotypical people meet autistic people, 'the disjuncture may be more severe for the non-autistic disposition as it is experienced as unusual, while for the autistic person it is a common experience' (Milton, 2012: 885). It is easy to see why from this vantage point – one steeped in majority privilege and a pathologising paradigm – these disjunctures might be thought of as an autistic problem. However, as we'll see, there is increasing evidence to support Milton's suggestion that the problem is one that runs both ways.

The double empathy problem: empirical evidence

Over the past decade, a rapidly growing number of research studies have either directly tested the double empathy problem hypothesis – and found evidence for it – or inadvertently demonstrated it in their results. Some have done so by illuminating the difficulties that non-autistic people also appear to experience in understanding autistic people: highlighting the two-way nature of the issues leading to communication breakdowns. Others have, instead, demonstrated the ways in which rapport and mutual understanding can flow with ease between autistic people, proving[39] that in the right circumstances, autistic people *are* capable of inferring

---

39 Not that we really should have needed research to prove this to us.

emotional states and communicating socially. We'll spend the rest of this chapter looking at some of these studies and thinking about what they tell us about the potential pitfalls in cross-neurotype communication...

Non-autistic difficulties reading autistic emotional states

We now have extensive evidence, for example, that non-autistic people experience difficulty in inferring the emotional and mental states of autistic people (e.g. Brewer *et al*, 2016; Edey *et al*, 2016; Heasman & Gillespie, 2018; Hubbard *et al*, 2017; Sheppard *et al*, 2016). In one such study, Brewer *et al* (2016) investigated the ability of non-autistic participants to identify the emotions of autistic participants, as conveyed via their facial expressions. Three posing conditions were set in which the 16 autistic and matched non-autistic control participants were asked to pose six basic emotions – happiness, sadness, fear, surprise, anger and disgust. In the first condition, they were asked to pose naturally, to the best of their ability, in the second, with the intention to communicate the emotion and in the third, with the benefit of a mirrored reflection of the posed expression. The third, mirrored condition was important for trying to offset any potential effects resulting from *alexithymia*.[40] In the emotion recognition phase, participants 14 autistic and 13 non-autistic control participants were asked to select which emotion matched the randomly presented series of facial expression images from the three posing conditions and to rate, on a scale of 1-9, how confident they felt in their judgement.

What Brewer and colleagues found, was that autistic facial expressions were more poorly identified than those posed by the non-autistic participants and that this remained the case for both autistic and non-autistic recogniser groups. Interestingly, facial expressions from both groups were better recognised when posed under the second (communicative) and third (mirrored) conditions. The original stance for this study was not especially neurodiversity-affirming; the intended aim of the study was to see whether autistic people were able to *produce* 'recognisable emotional expressions' (Brewer *et al*, 2016: 262) and the researchers ultimately concluded that autistic people could not. However,

---

40 Alexithymia is a condition in which individuals struggle to identify their own emotions or distinguish interoceptive bodily signals (such as hunger, thirst, pressure, etc) and is present in up to 50 percent of autistic people (see Bird *et al*, 2010; Brewer *et al*, 2016; Garfinkel *et al* 2016).

viewed from a slightly different angle, these findings demonstrate the difficulty non-autistic people may have interpreting the facial expressions of autistic people.

In a similar kind of study, Sheppard *et al* (2015) sought to test whether non-autistic people were able to interpret the behaviour of autistic people. Twenty young autistic males and 20 young non-autistic males (mean age of 15 years) were surreptitiously recorded reacting to one of four scenarios. Having been told they were coming to pose facial expressions for a subsequent study when they first entered the room – where the camera was set up and already secretly filming – the researcher performed one of four scenarios: either telling a joke, telling a story, making the participant wait or giving them three compliments. In the first study, 30 non-autistic raters (15 female, 15 male, with a mean age of 23 years), watched short clips of the participant reactions before having to select which scenario they believed them to be responding to. In the second study, 20 different non-autistic raters (ten female, ten male, mean age of 20 years) watched the same reaction clips without being informed of the scenario conditions they were responding to, and rated each according to expressiveness on a seven-point scale. Raters were not informed that some of the participants they would be watching were autistic.

In the first study, for the story, waiting, and compliment conditions, rater judgements 'effectively (and unwittingly) discriminated' between autistic participants (Shepherd *et al*, 2015: 1250). In other words, they routinely found autistic reactions harder than non-autistic reactions to match with the correct conditions. In the second study (in which viewers had to rate expressiveness) no differences were observed between the autistic and non-autistic groups apart from in the compliment condition[41], leading the researchers to conclude that, despite autistic participants 'being expressive in most cases, it seems that the form of their expressions were not easily interpretable to participants and perhaps were atypical' (Shepherd *et al*, 2015: 1251).

---

41 In their discussion of the results, the researchers puzzle over why the autistic group should be less expressive in response to being paid a compliment. *Camouflaging* or *masking* (see Pearson & Rose, 2023) is a strategy often adopted by autistic people in social situations, whereby their natural responses and behaviours are suppressed and reactions that are considered more socially acceptable or less socially risky are performed. It strikes me that a group of autistic adolescent males, the likes of whom typically find themselves at the periphery of society and at significantly increased risk of being bullied (Zablotsky *et al*, 2014), might be unaccustomed to receiving compliments and be unsure of how they 'should' respond.

Finally, a piece of research by Heasman and Gillespie (2018) discovered something interesting about autistic perspective-taking that also supports the double empathy problem theory. The aim of this study was to try to identify and understand the potential effects of cultural representations surrounding Asperger's syndrome on the social relationships of autistic adults with such a diagnosis. In order to do this, the researchers devised a methodology that could map out misunderstandings between pairs of individuals using something called the *Interpersonal Perception Method (IPM)*: originally devised by Laing *et al* (1966) to probe interpersonal disagreements, often used in couples' therapy.

In this study, 22 pairs were recruited to take part, with each pair comprising one autistic adult (with a mean age of 21 years) and a chosen (non-autistic) family member. Both participants in each pair were provided with a set of 12 topics commonly understood to be challenging for autistic people (e.g. 'small talk', 'handling everyday tasks', 'making decisions', etc.) and asked to perform three ratings for each topic using a six-point scale. The first rating for each topic was a self-rating (i.e. how good am I at small talk/managing everyday tasks etc.). The second was an other-rating (i.e. how good is my partner at small talk/managing everyday tasks etc.), and the third was a meta-rating (i.e. how will my partner rate me at small talk/managing everyday tasks etc). After giving their ratings, participants were recorded reflecting on their decisions.

Firstly, Heasman and Gillespie found that, overall, 'misunderstandings occur on both sides of the relationship' (2018: 5). Secondly, when it came to the self-ratings, autistic participants rated themselves, on average, more poorly across all tasks compared to the self-ratings of their non-autistic family members. However, in the other-ratings, non-autistic family members rated the autistic participants as markedly more poorly still (i.e. potentially underestimating the abilities of the autistic adults). Most significant was the fact that in the meta-ratings, autistic participants accurately predicted the poor, lower rating of them given by their family members *despite not agreeing with it*.

What this demonstrates is a highly sophisticated level of meta-perspective-taking that challenges the theory of mind deficit theory of autism. Ironically, and sadly, when the reasons for the given ratings were analysed, they revealed that family members tended to be focused on the perceived 'extreme impairment in social understanding' (2018: 8) of their autistic family member: beliefs that ultimately interfered with their ability (or willingness) to 'consider more nuanced aspects' of the autistic person's behaviour' (*Ibid*). In addition, it was the autistic participants who showed the greatest tendency to consider themselves as the cause of misunderstandings (62% vs 40% of non-autistic family members).

Together these studies begin to form a body of evidence to support the idea, felt in the bones of many autistic people, that the lack of understanding between autistic and non-autistic people runs both ways.

Non-autistic people judging autistic people negatively

One related area of research that highlights the significant role of the non-autistic party in cross-neurotype interactions is the growing body of studies revealing the negative first impressions about autistic people that non-autistic people seem to form (e.g. Cage & Burton, 2019; Cola *et al*, 2020; Morrison *et al*, 2019a; Sasson *et al*, 2017).

One such piece of research is that undertaken by Sasson and colleagues (2017) which sought to identify the extent to which the perceptions, behaviours and social decisions of non-autistic interlocutors affect the social difficulties observed in cross-neurotype interactions. Forty participants (20 autistic and 20 matched non-autistic participants) were filmed engaging in a 'high risk social challenge task' (Sasson *et al*, 2017: 2): a mock audition for a reality show. The first ten seconds of footage from each participant were then edited to generate five different 'presentation modalities'. The first presentation modality was audio only (i.e. a ten-second audio recording of the participant undertaking the task). The second was visual only (i.e. a ten-second video clip with no audio). The third was audio-visual (i.e. a video clip including the related sound recording) and the fourth was a single static image – but not one that was taken mid-speech or mid-gesture. The fifth and final modality was a written transcript of speech content from the first ten seconds.

Two hundred and fourteen undergraduates (with a mean age of 21 years) were recruited as raters and were charged with rating one presentation modality per each participant on a scale of 0-3, according to ten criteria. The first six criteria – attractiveness, awkwardness, intelligence, likeability, trustworthiness, and dominance/submissiveness – are all associated with forming first impressions. The additional four criteria –

willingness to live near the participant, likelihood of hanging out with them in the rater's free time, level of comfort sitting next to them, and likelihood of starting a conversation with them – were included to reflect behavioural intentions.

For all of the presentation modalities – except for the written transcripts – the autistic participants were rated significantly more negatively than the non-autistic participants. These negative ratings of autistic participants were exacerbated in the audio-visual modality (as compared to the audio-only modality), whereas for the non-autistic group, when visuals were added to the audio the ratings became more favourable. Most significant, then, was the discovery that the 'biases disappear when impressions are based on conversational content lacking audio-visual cues, suggesting that style, not substance, drives negative impressions of [autism]' (Sasson et al, 2017: 1).

It is not *what* is said that triggers an unfavourable judgement by non-autistic people, nor even necessarily *how* it is said (although atypical prosody clearly also plays an important role as we've seen in Chapter 5). Negative first impressions are, instead, formed instantly on the basis of seemingly imperceptible visual cues that suggest that the autistic person is somehow *other*. This is important knowledge, because if non-autistic people are entering into conversations with autistic people – consciously or unconsciously – with their hackles raised, how much of a 'helpful speaker' (Van Der Henst et al, 2002 and Chapter 3) are they likely to be?

Autistic sociality and interpersonal attunement

A lot of research undertaken recently has started showing us what autistic people have been saying for a long time: that they *do* often experience high levels of mutual understanding and rapport, but that this often comes more easily when interacting with other autistic and neurodivergent individuals (Crompton et al, 2019a; 2019b; Crompton et al, 2020; Heasman & Gillespie, 2019; Morrison et al, 2019b; Williams et al, 2021).

In one study, researchers Crompton, Fletcher-Watson and Ropar (2019b) hypothesised that if the common belief that autism is characterised by social communication deficits were true, an *information transfer task* – one involving the passing of information from one person to another – should be significantly impaired when autistic people are providing the information. In order to test this theory, they devised a task involving a diffusion chain[42] where a story told to an original participant is recounted to each subsequent participant by the previous one, for eight iterations. The activity was designed so that chains would involve three pairing conditions: the first with pairs of exclusively autistic participants, the second with exclusively non-autistic pairs and the third with a mix of (alternating) autistic and non-autistic individuals. The story told to the first participant in the diffusion chain by the researcher involved 30 distinct points and featured the adventures of a bear on a surreal journey.

They found, as the double empathy problem might predict, that the detail retention across autistic chains did not differ from that of the non-autistic chains, but that it *did* decline more steeply in the cross-neurotype, mixed chains. In other words, communication flowed more efficaciously within matched-neurotype pairings. The reduction in the quality of information transfer in the mixed pair groups also ran in parallel with a reduction in rapport, which had been measured on leaving the room using a 100-point scale with five dimensions: ease, enjoyment, success, friendliness, and awkwardness.

In another study, Heasman and Gillespie (2019) sought to investigate the manner in which a group entirely made up of autistic people might interact with one another. In particular, they were interested in how autistic people build social understanding given that often in research 'methods for investigating autistic sociality tend to assume neurotypical definitions of being social' (Heasman and Gillespie, 2019: 910). The researchers video-recorded the interactions of 30 adult autistic participants across 20 sessions (with ten participants taking part in multiple sessions), playing video games together on an Xbox One in groups of between two and five at a local autism support charity. The conversational turns (i.e. the back-and-forth utterances) within the transcribed interactions were then scored according to three criteria: *affect* (i.e. the harmony of displayed emotion between the turn, *symmetry* (how assertive or submissive a turn was in relation to the previous turn) and *coherence* (the extent to which a turn stays roughly on topic).

In their analysis, the authors identified two seemingly unique features of autistic intersubjectivity. The first was an apparent 'generous assumption of common ground that, when understood, led to rapid rapport, and, when

---

[42] Diffusion chains are common conversational games, particularly for children. The most well-known example is called 'Telephone', in which a message is whispered from one person to the next, with the final version spoken aloud and compared to the original.

not understood, resulted in potentially disruptive utterance' (Heasman & Gillespie, 2019: 910). This was demonstrated in 'sudden and specific topic shifts' (Heasman & Gillespie, 2019: 915), sometimes involving a shift into the impersonated voice of a fictional character. These digressions into another voice were not explained, nor was their comprehension or recognition checked at the time: which the authors took as indicating implicit assumptions that they were shared knowledge. It is also possible that these repetitious fragments are a type of echolalia. As well as the players assuming access to a shared repertoire of impressions and cultural representations, it is also possible that these switches are unguarded (or, un-'masked') autistic auditory-stim behaviours with the intention being more to play, rather than to convey.

The second unique feature was 'a low demand for coordination that ameliorated many challenges associated with disruptive turns' (Heasman & Gillespie, 2019: 910). In line with a potential linguistic playfulness in the autistic interactions, the authors note that while generous assumptions of common ground could sometimes fracture coherence, at 'other times it could spark creative, productive and affective passages of dialogue' (Heasman & Gillespie, 2019: 915.). Moreover, the lower demand for coordination 'ameliorated many challenges associated with disruptive turns' (Heasman & Gillespie, 2019: 910). It is possible that this pattern of communicating – with its sudden leaps and turns, intrusions and tolerance of disjunctures – may reflect a lifetime of experiencing interaction as a neuro-minority, unable to easily predict what is coming next yet needing to be ready to *go on*.

Findings from a different study by Crompton, Fletcher-Watson and Ropar (2019a) seem to corroborate this interpretation of a less constrained form of interacting that can emerge between autistic interlocutors. In this study, autistic adults were asked, through semi-structured interviews, to describe the experiences of the relationships they have with both autistic and non-autistic family and friends. In addition to reporting a tendency towards practical and affective difficulties with cross-neurotype interactions, autistic respondents described 'feelings of comfort and ease' (Crompton *et al*, 2019a: 8) during the time spent with autistic companions:

> '*Many stated that communication styles were similar between autistic people, and this made interactions more comfortable, that*

it was easier to follow conversations and understand what people mean:

"With autistic people, I have a much better idea of what people are doing, what they mean, and picking up on things" – Participant 2

Participants noted that there is flexibility with their autistic friends and family about what constitutes a "good" interaction, and that there is a shared understanding that if there is a problem during an interaction that there will be understanding from their autistic family and friends.'

(Crompton et al, 2019a: 8)

The low demand for coordination that Heasman and Gillespie found is reminiscent of something mentioned by Ochs and Solomon (2005) in a report on their linguistic anthropological work with a large dataset of transcribed conversations involving autistic children. They noted that the autistic child participants in the project often made contributions to an ongoing conversation that did not entirely coordinate with what had gone before:

'Neither wholly irrelevant nor wholly relevant, such structures are what we call proximally relevant to the social practice underway.'

(Ochs & Solomon, 2005: 143)

The authors found that the autistic children often responded to opinions, or emotional or ironic comments from their adult conversational partners in two ways: either by making their interactional contribution 'locally relevant to what was just said or what just transpired, but not to the more extensive concern or enterprise under consideration', or by shifting 'the focus away from personal states and situations to topically relevant impersonal, objective cultural knowledge' (Ochs & Solomon, 2005: 158). In this way, the children were participating in the back-and-forth of talk-in-interaction, but through contributions that are not directly on topic. This 'proximal relevance' may well be explainable by a lower autistic requirement for tight coordination and conversational coherence.

Finally, some of my own research also adds to the growing picture of autistic sociality. For this study, we (Williams *et al*, 2021) organised a pilot community engagement project around the topic of local loneliness (Williams, 2020), where a mix of autistic and non-autistic people were invited to come and talk in pairs (for around ten minutes per conversation) about the issue. While autistic experiences of loneliness were a genuine source of interest (and later analysed and reported on as a secondary study -see Quadt, Williams *et al*, 2023), for the main study we were more interested in *how* pairs of individuals – featuring a minimum of one autistic person – did or didn't achieve mutual understanding during these recorded and transcribed conversations. The project involved eight core autistic participants (three male, five female): each having three short conversations. The first was with a familiar, chosen, conversation partner (e.g. a family member, friend or colleague), the second with an autistic stranger (i.e. one of the other participants), and the final conversation was with a non-autistic stranger.

Based on the double empathy problem theory, I expected to find that mutual understanding would be hardest to achieve in the cross-neurotype pairs, and based on relevance theory (and its ideas around shared cognitive environments) that familiarity with one's conversation partner would improve mutual understanding in cross-neurotype communication. In many ways, this did bear out. All five matched-neurotype conversations (featuring two autistic participants) seemed to be characterised by a significant and sometimes dramatic increase in flow (e.g. smoothness of turn-taking), rapport and intersubjective attunement: even though in all but one case these pairings were strangers to one another. There was sometimes more flow, rapport and mutual understanding in these conversations than when autistic people spoke with non-autistic friends or family members they knew well, and in some cases, autistic people who had difficulties with speaking (like stuttering, forgetting words or saying wrong words) had fewer of these problems when talking with other autistic people.

However, what we also found was that, in fact, *all* of the conversations across *all* the pairing types seemed to have good levels of apparent mutual understanding with very few to no misunderstandings. There were also some instances where cross-neurotype pairs appeared to achieve high levels of interpersonal attunement, rapport and mutual understanding. This was something of a surprise and is not what traditional autism theories would predict. We wondered if it may be that the topic of loneliness helped to create an affective common ground where people had similar experiences to share, making it easier to connect. Essentially, what this showed us was that given the right circumstances, not only can autistic sociality flourish, but cross-neurotype communication too.

Chapter 7: Mind the gap

'It takes more work to communicate with someone whose native language isn't the same as yours. And autism goes deeper than language and culture; autistic people are 'foreigners' in any society. You're going to have to give up your assumptions about shared meanings. You're going to have to learn to back up to levels more basic than you've probably thought about before, to translate, and to check to make sure your translations are understood. You're going to have to give up the certainty that comes of being on your own familiar territory, of knowing you're in charge...'
Jim Sinclair, autistic autism-rights activist, 1993: 2)

All communication involves some kind of transmission from one mind to another, some kind of mental broadcasting. In many cases, this transmission also requires an act of translation: translation of ideas and concepts, code-switching[43], or conversion into a different language entirely. We are constantly monitoring and adapting our communication to tailor it (to the best of our abilities) to the person or people we're addressing. However, one of the things about being around people with whom we share a lot of common ground – or, in relevance-theoretic terms, with whom large portions of our cognitive environments overlap – is that less energy and effort is required to shape and translate our utterances. When we're with people similar to ourselves, they often *just get it*.

In the previous chapter, we looked in detail at the theory of the double empathy problem: the idea that communication between two 'differently disposed social actors' (Milton, 2012: 884) may more easily fall short, on account of the larger distance between perspectives. Essentially, the greater the gap between *dispositions*, the harder mutual understanding is likely to be.

There are a number of theories and concepts from adjacent disciplines that parallel or speak to this double empathy problem. While not all of

---

43 Code switching refers to the adjustments in speech style, expression, syntax and vocabulary made (consciously or unconsciously) by those from minority groups in order to be accepted by a dominant culture – a practice often undertaken by Black people in white-dominant, Global North settings.

them directly address cross-neurotype communication or communication with autistic people, they are useful elements in the picture we're building about understanding others – especially those who are more different to ourselves – in a neurodiverse world.

This chapter will spend a little bit of time exploring some of these. Firstly, we'll look at some theories and approaches that are interested in how similarity and difference affect interaction and understanding, including *Mind-space*, the *dialectical misattunement hypothesis and participatory sense-making*. Finally, we'll take a short detour around the way English is used as Lingua Franca between speakers from sometimes very different cultural backgrounds, and how that might provide a potential working model of communication across dispositional gaps.

Mind-space

As we saw in Chapter 2, theory of mind has long been understood to be the main mechanism by which humans can mind-read others. Yet, as we've also seen, proficiency in theory of mind can vary dramatically from person to person, and from context to context. Coming from the fields of cognitive neuroscience and psychology, a collective of researchers (Conway *et al*, 2019) have proposed the idea of Mind-space as a means of trying to explain these evident differences in the accuracy of mental state inferences. The hypothesis behind the Mind-space model was that the accuracy of such inferences 'can be explained by the ability to characterise the mind giving rise to the mental state' (Conway *et al*, 2019: 2). In other words, we have a representation (or, characterisation) of the rough (known) shape of another person's mind within our own: kind of akin to a 360-degree image of them as a thinking being projected onto the back wall of our mind's eye. We have a sense of who they are and, to an extent, how their mind will work. So far, so good.

Mind-space takes its structure from the existing concept of *Face-space*: a psychological model that seeks to explain how we process and store the facial information used for facial recognition. Face-space – like Mind-space – is a theoretical, multidimensional cognitive space (i.e. bit of our mind) against which dimensions of individual faces (such as face shape, distance between the eyes, age, sex/gender signifiers, distinguishing features) are plotted and represented (Valentine, 1991). As such, Mind-space is seen as a set of vectors reflecting 'any characteristic of minds that allows them to be individuated' (Conway *et al*, 2019: 2).

Conway and *et al* (2019) hypothesise that the more accurately we are able to plot another's mind within our Mind-space, the more attuned our inferences about said mind will be:

> *'Crucially, minds moderate the link between situational contexts and the mental states they evoke: two different target minds in the same situation may generate completely different mental states. The accuracy with which those target minds can be represented, therefore, is likely to contribute to accuracy in inferring the target's mental states.'*
>
> (Conway *et al*, 2019: 2).

Suspicious minds

An example of how this might be so is given in a slightly earlier paper by Conway, Catmur and Bird (2019). The researchers first draw the important distinction between theory of mind ability – the ability to *represent* mental states – and what it is that empirical theory of mind measures tend to test – namely the ability to make accurate mental state inferences. What this distinction means is that a participant in a test may have the ability to represent the mental state of another perfectly well, yet still draw incorrect inferences.

Turning to the famous Sally-Anne 'false belief' test we looked at in Chapter 2, the researchers question how the results may be affected if Sally (the character returning to look for her ball/doll/bottle of champagne) is known to be highly suspicious. In such an instance, it is quite possible that a participant who 'has a dimension of suspiciousness in their Mind-space and who recognizes that Sally is at the extreme end of this dimension' (i.e. also very suspicious: Conway *et al*, 2019: 803) may fare better in correctly anticipating Sally's actions, than a participant who either has a weak suspicion dimension or inaccurately places Sally along the continuum.

The researchers break this down further by imagining two types of participants and two different scenarios. In the first scenario, what the researchers have called an 'average participant' is likely to place Sally at the population average of suspiciousness in their Mind-space. From here, they will probably expect Sally to think that her treasure is where she left it. In the second scenario, the researchers imagine that this average participant has prior knowledge that Sally has high levels of suspiciousness. Here they surmise that the participant will represent Sally at a higher vector of suspiciousness in their Mind-space, further from the average, with the result of representing Sally as suspecting that Anne has moved her treasure. The second participant in this thought experiment has been exposed to an untrustworthy population. It is therefore possible that they may have a suspiciousness vector higher than the population average in their Mind-space and, in the first scenario with no additional information, assume Sally sees the world similarly and also represent Sally as believing that Anne may have hidden her treasure. Finally, in the second scenario, having prior knowledge that Sally has high levels of suspiciousness, this second participant will likely represent Sally even further from their average, and imagine that Sally holds the belief that Anne has absolutely stolen her treasure.

The important difference between these scenarios, here, is the type of population to which participants had been exposed before taking part in the study, i.e., the kinds of minds they had already encountered. According to Conway and colleagues (2019: 50), 'locating another mind within Mind-space may depend upon the particular mind to be modelled and its relationship to the kinds of minds one has previously encountered which have shaped one's Mind-space'. The impact of this is significant. It is both one's own Mind-space shape and the Mind-spaces of those with whom one comes into contact, particularly in formative years, that defines the parameters of one's mapping of the potentiality of other minds.

The implication this has for atypical minds is also significant, as the authors recognise:

> *'The idea that one's theory of mind ability may depend on the target mind to be represented has interesting implications for atypical groups. Neurotypical participants may perform well on existing theory of mind tasks in which the 'correct' answers are derived by neurotypical consensus... as their own mind is similar to the average. Conversely, neurotypical participants may also have minds that are particularly easy to represent by the majority of the population.*

> *In contrast, those who have atypical minds may find it harder to represent the minds of neurotypical individuals, and in turn, be harder for neurotypical individuals to represent.'*
>
> (Conway *et al*, 2019: 51)

This certainly supports the findings from research investigating the double empathy problem that demonstrate how sharing (or not sharing) a neurotype has a great bearing on the success of interactions. If Mind-space theory is correct, we first need exposure to and interaction with minds that are markedly different to our own in order to be able to start representing them in our Mind-space. Only once we have a pre-existing sense of how *this kind of mind* works will we be able to properly infer its mental states: something which – as we've seen in earlier chapters – is essential not only for rapport and intersubjective connection, but for interpreting meaning and basic understanding. There's something of a Catch-22 here about neurodivergent people being neuro-minorities that needs some further thought if we are to find ways to better support mutual understanding and connectivity.

Dialectical misattunement hypothesis

One further theory addressing the breakdowns in understanding that can occur in cross-neurotype communication and that runs in parallel with the double empathy problem is the *dialectical misattunement hypothesis* (Bolis *et al*, 2017). The dialectical misattunement hypothesis draws on a blend of socio-cultural theories, enactivism (see Chapter 1) and *Bayesian accounts of brain function* (or, theories of *'predictive processing'*). The Bayesian brain and predictive processing are big topics that require whole books of their own[44] – and which we don't have room here to go into in great depth – but a short summary should be enough to contextualise what Bolis and colleagues have to say about cross-neurotype communication.

The Bayesian brain and predictive processing

Traditionally – within Western/Global Northen philosophical traditions – perception has been conceptualised as functioning from the bottom up, or from the outside inwards. Our sensory organs were thought of as receiving signs and signals from our environment (e.g. visual information that can

---

[44] If interested, you'd do well to try *Surfing Uncertainty: Prediction, action, and the embodied mind* by Andy Clark (2015).

be received through the eyes and interpreted as colour and shape, which in turn can be interpreted as a great oak tree standing before us). The world was 'out there', and our sensorium processed the data conveyed to us via our sensory organs to inform us of how it looked/smelt/sounded. And yet, numerous sensory peculiarities and seeming miswirings – such as common optical illusions and the famous 'rubber hand illusion'[45] (Botvinick & Cohen, 1998) – seemed to evade this means of explanation. Predictive processing is a more recent theory[46] that flips the order of events and places the brain at the centre of perception, as an organ of inference that actively constructs what it perceives.

As a means of most efficiently managing the impossibly vast and constant stream of continuously churning environmental and interoceptive data, the brain reduces its load by generating informed predictions (called *priors*) about its surroundings. Reality and perception, essentially, are tightly controlled hallucinations, with the brain constantly working to minimise errors in its predictions by paying attention only to anomalous perceptual data that don't match its predictions. These prediction errors are fed back up to either tweak the signal (e.g. it's not an oak tree, it's a man in a tree costume) or trigger an action response to right the mismatch (e.g. I've picked up a cup I thought was cool. It is, in fact, scalding hot, so I'll let go). Because the generation of these priors depends on estimations of both the state of the world and, to an extent, of our individual sensory uncertainty (i.e. how accurate is the sensory information I'm receiving), they are ultimately *probabilistic beliefs*, hence the discussion of the *Bayesian*[47] *brain* and the statistical basis of predictive coding (see: Friston, 2003).

Predictive processing and autism

In the last decade, several accounts have emerged that attempt to describe autism from a predictive processing perspective. Pellicano and Burr (2012), for example, hypothesised that *hypo-priors* – i.e. weaker strength Bayesian

---

[45] In the *rubber hand illusion* experiments, participants are asked to place one hand on the table before them and hide the other from sight. A rubber hand is placed in the position on the table where the hidden hand would naturally sit. Both the hidden hand and the rubber hand are simultaneously stroked – with something like a small paint brush. Generally, participants experience a sensation of embodied ownership over the seen, rubber hand, and disembodiment of the hidden hand in an experience sometimes called 'proprioceptive drift'.

[46] Although, Prussian philosopher Hermann von Helmholtz offered up a comparable outside-in theory of perception in the mid-1800s.

[47] Bayesian modelling is a statistical method of assigning probabilities to problems to update prior beliefs in light of new information – more or less: I am in no way a mathematician.

predictions – may lead to a greater reliance on real-time, bottom-up, sensory input: making autistic perception potentially both more accurate and also more overwhelming.

In a proposed refinement of Pellicano and Burr's (2012) theory, Friston, Lawson and Frith (2013) suggested that it was likely the *precision weighting* (i.e. the allocation of how 'newsworthy' the beliefs are (Friston, 2016: 2)) given to prior beliefs that is atypical for autistic people, not a weakness in the priors themselves.

So far, the majority of the discussion has remained largely speculative and has tended to rely on the language of deficit (e.g. there is a 'failure' of Bayesian inference, a 'disfunction' in the brain, an 'inflexibility' around tolerating ambiguity). It is interesting to ponder whether – as with the monotropic account of autism, where human attention allocation is seen to be 'normally distributed' and 'genetically determined' (Murray *et al*, 2005: 140) – there might be an evolutionarily derived, normal human range of wider or narrower precision weighting of priors, with autistic people tending to fall to one end (resulting in more accurate sensory perception tempered by a propensity to become easily overwhelmed)? For our purposes, the TLDR version is: autistic people may have slightly different recipes in their predictive processing.

Dialectical misattunements

Returning to the *dialectical misattunement hypothesis*, Bolis and colleagues (2017) have taken a predictive processing account of intersubjectivity and applied it, specifically, to cross-neurotype intersubjectivity. In essence, the view is that the socio-communicative issues that have traditionally been thought of arising as some inherent consequence of being autistic should instead be thought of as – at least in part – emanating from a 'cumulative misattunement between persons' (Bolis *et al*, 2017: 359). *Misattunements*, here, are described here as 'disturbances of the dynamic and reciprocal unfolding of an interaction across multiple time scales' (2017: 355). In simpler terms, lots of small misalignments of body language, linguistic cues, opinions and perspectives culminate in a lack of *interpersonal attunement* (see Chapter 2).

Central to this theory is a *dialectical* view of (what the authors have described as) 'psychiatric' conditions, including autism. In other words, it draws on a perspective that takes account of the way that seemingly opposing ideas or ways of being connect or conflict and ultimately shape one another. An equally important component of the dialectical misattunement hypothesis is the premise that interpersonal attunement has a significant role in forming the individual self[48]. As such, and as with the double empathy problem, it is not simply the case that one 'disordered mind' is generating discord within an interaction, but rather that there is 'a dynamic interpersonal mismatch' (*Ibid*) between two apparently incompatible ways of being.

According to the originators of the hypothesis, two interrelated processes may be occurring that result in the frequent misunderstandings between autistic and non-autistic people. On the one hand, misalignments in communication can be seen as resulting from 'increasingly divergent predictive and (inter-)action styles across individuals' (Bolis *et al*, 2017: 369). Micro differences in predictive processing styles, such as described above (which, in turn, shape divergent perspectives and ways of being) set autistic and non-autistic apart, in a similar view to that of the double empathy problem. With divergent ways of experiencing and processing information in interaction, markers of interpersonal attunement (such as body language synchrony) in cross-neurotype pairings become harder to achieve, thus creating a growing sense of misattunement.

On the other hand, the authors suggest that, as a consequence of regularly experiencing interpersonal misattunements as a neuro-minority within a neurotypically-dominant society, autistic people may experience a pattern of social exclusion across development that results in 'impoverished opportunities for acquiring socio-culturally mediated knowledge and skills' (Ibid). I'm not so sure that (especially in our now hyper-connected world with its bombardment of all kinds of media) it's quite right to say that autistic people routinely miss out on opportunities to learn the social and cultural knowledge needed to be able to participate properly in fulfilling social interactions. What I do think the authors get right, however, is the role of social exclusion and stigma in exacerbating social isolation (more on that in Chapter 9).

Participatory sense-making

Another interesting and parallel framework that speaks, in part, to cross-neurotype interaction is the idea of *participatory sense-making* (Cuffari

---

48 For more on this, see Vygotsky (1978).

et al, 2015; De Jaegher, 2013; De Jaegher & Di Paolo, 2008; Di Paolo *et al*, 2018).

As with the dialectical misattunement hypothesis, there is a lot of theoretical detail underpinning the concept of participatory sense-making[49] which draws on some of the ideas we looked at in Chapter 1. Situated within an embodied, enactivist view of cognition, *sense-making* describes the ways in which a cognisor (i.e. a cognitive being) engages in an embodied activity within (and along with) its environment. Alternatively put, 'sense-making is the capacity of an autonomous system to adaptively regulate its operation and its relation to the environment depending on the virtual consequences for its own viability as a form of life' (Di Paolo *et al*, 2018: 33). A cognising organism (such as we are) needs to be able to tune in to its ever-changing environment (which includes, of course, other cognising beings) and moderate the ways in which in interacts in order to stay alive and well. So far (perhaps a bit abstract, but), so good...

Thinking specifically about humans this way, we might best be described as 'organic, sensorimotor, intersubjective' – as well as linguistic – bodies (Di Paolo *et al*, 2018: 2)[50]. When our sense-making interacts with other human sense-makers and, crucially, is 'performed socially or enacted as a shared practice' (Di Paolo *et al*, 2018: 74) it becomes a *participatory* act involving two linguistic bodies. Communication, here, should be thought of as something that is taking place between two, coupled, embodied agents, both assisting in the sense-making of the other. Individual cognition and meaning-making involves, and are to an extent contingent on, the activity of others.

When it is successful, communication – an intersubjective engagement between agents – can be experienced as 'fluctuating feelings of connectedness with an other, including that of being in the flow of an interaction' (De Jaegher, 2013: 6). A lack of success – or communication breakdown – however, does not mean that participatory sense-making isn't taking place. In fact, the presence of precarity in an interaction is part of what drives the participatory sense-making activity:

---

49 Too much for here, but if you're curious, try *Linguistic Bodies* by Di Paolo, Cuffari, and De Jaegher (2018).
50 In a similar – if slightly more delicate – epithet to Andy Clark's (2015) description of humans as *meat that predicts*.

> 'When sense-makers engage in social interaction, it is the
> intertwining vulnerabilities of interaction and participants that make
> possible the ongoing and various transformations of sense-making.
> This does not mean that actual breakdown must be present in each
> and every interaction, but that without the possibility and risk of
> breakdown, there is no participatory sense-making. Breakdowns are
> not mere obstacles to social understanding that must be overcome,
> but lie at its root, even when interactions go smoothly.'
>
> (Di Paolo et al, 2018: 75)

While the ever-present threat of instability drives embodied agents to enact sense-making – including with others in the form of participatory sense-making – difficulties with interpersonal attunement can still trouble a paring's ability to *coordinate* its interaction. Within this framework, *coordination* refers to the intentional, coregulated coupling of two cognising agents. In instances involving pairings whose embodied experiences differ dramatically, interpersonal attunement and coordination may prove more problematic:

> 'Sensorimotor differences, especially those involving temporal aspects
> of perception and movement, will affect interaction and coordination
> in social encounters, and therefore introduce systematic differences in
> participatory sense-making.'
>
> (De Jaegher, 2013: 11)

Because of this, the theorists behind participatory sense-making have thought in some depth about autistic sense-making and how that plays out within cross-neurotype participatory sense-making couplings. Addressing the issue of apparent communication difficulties, often thought to be experienced by autistic speakers (but, according to the double empathy problem in fact experienced by both parties), the authors propose the following hypothesis. Because of their divergent sensory attunements to the world, and the resultingly divergent experiences of social interaction, autistic people, they suggest, may 'cope with the inherent tensions of participatory sense-making between individual and interactive norms by either overregulating or underregulating [the coupling]' (Di Paolo et al, 2018: 266). In other words, autistic people may adopt different strategies – at a pre-reflective, embodied level – in response to points of tension or evolving misunderstanding that, in turn, aren't recognised or understood by their neurotypical interaction partner.

In summary

Mind-space framework, the dialectic misattunement hypothesis and participatory sense-making each draw on slightly different systems of thinking about how individuals make sense of and interact with others. However, common to them all is an awareness that where there is a difference in how our minds are organised and how they process information – usually understood to have an embodied basis – mutual understanding is harder to achieve. In that way, each of these theories accords with the double empathy problem and the idea that difficulties in mutual understanding between people of different neurotypes run in both directions.

Does that mean that cross-neurotype interactions are simply doomed to go poorly, due to the innate, embodied differences enacted over the course of lifetimes that set us down different cognitive pathways? Not necessarily. Cross-neurotype families, friendships, romantic relationships and workplaces exist all around us and sometimes work really well. There's also one really quite sizeable example of interactions that take place every day between people from differing dispositions (if not neurotypes) that might help us think about what helps us bridge those gaps, namely, English as a Lingua Franca…

English as a Lingua Franca as a working model of cross-dispositional communication

Every morning I'd screech down the steep residential road, one hand invariably holding the croissant I was trying to stuff into my mouth, the other gripping the bike brake, and arrive, pink-cheeked from the wind outside the tall Georgian building. I'd hurriedly climb a series of narrowing, carpeted staircases, pushing through weighted doors with books and scissors and piles of papers balanced against my chest and under my chin, and set up the room ready for the small groups of professionals who had travelled from Europe, South America, Japan, or Russia to 'perfect' their Business English.

Something different was happening in these small rooms... different to any other English class I'd taught before. Traditional measures of linguistic ability seemed to matter less for these speakers whose English mediated their day-to-day professional activities. Here were experts in their own fields, using sometimes very 'broken', simple English to navigate complex interactions or negotiate contracts. The ones who were most communicatively successful were those who were able to... to what? I didn't really have a word for it...

Something about receptivity and reciprocity. Something about humour (my donkey-laughter at their jokes would ricochet out into the corridor, bouncing off chrome-framed prints of the pier, raising an eyebrow of my boss in his far office). Something about expanding themselves... over the linguistic, the cultural, the cognitive gaps that stood between them and their interlocutor... Something about English as a Lingua Franca.

English as a Lingua Franca

'ELF is not a thing, it is a way.'

(Sifakis & Bayyurt, 2018)

In part because it is the language of colonisers, and in part because of its dominance in popular media, English is currently the world's 'primary language for international communication' (Kinnock, in Graddol, 2006: 3) and particularly so for business and trade (Jenkins *et al*, 2011). The current working figure for the number of English speakers around the world was set around a decade and a half ago at approximately two billion (Crystal, 2008) – though this has likely since grown. Of that two billion, it is non-native speakers of English who are the most prolific: outnumbering native speakers at a ratio of at least three to one (Ibid). In other words, English is used most often around the world between speakers for whom it is a second (or third, or fourth) language and it is this usage context we're referring to when we talk about English being used as a *Lingua Franca*.

English is just one of many lingua francas currently or previously in use, though due to its breadth of geographical spread and its use across such a multiplicity of domains it has become the most dominant globally. As such, we now have vast and varied corpora (i.e. collections of transcribed linguistic data) of English as a Lingua Franca in use and a lot of work has been done to analyse its specific characteristics, particularly in the ways that they might differ from native-speaker English usage. Although we can't really describe English as a Lingua Franca as a *variation* of English in the typical sense (e.g. like *Chinglish* – the formal name for the Chinese English variation, or *Singlish* – Singaporean English, which each has unique and definable phonological, lexical and syntactic features[51]), English as a Lingua Franca does appear to possess its own identifiable qualities. In that sense, this is another way in which English as a Lingua Franca is something of a unique language case, as rather than being a specific linguistic system that can be learned, it is more of 'a communicative mode or situation' (Hall, 2018:75).

What is most interesting about English as a Lingua Franca, for our purposes, is its role as a highly successful mode of communication between speakers with sometimes dramatically divergent cognitive environments (shaped by different language and cultural backgrounds). Even when shared linguistic resources are low, rapport and essential comprehension can often be high, as I'd discovered in the Business English classrooms. What is it about the way English is used in these liminal, inherently cross-cultural encounters that facilitates this mutual understanding and are any of its characteristics transferrable to cross-neurotype communication?

Consensually non-normative
English is used as a Lingua Franca across a range of contexts (e.g. in international business, in academia, for social purposes) between speakers who do not share a first language. Being so intrinsically intercultural, 'common ground cannot be presumed and diversity needs to be negotiated

---

51 Phonology, lexis and syntax – i.e. the sounds and pronunciations, vocabulary and grammar.

locally' (Cogo, 2009: 254). In other words, speakers bring with them a range of differing cultural associations and socio-linguistic repertoires that need to be navigated each time any new pair of speakers interact.

As such, English as a Lingua Franca is often described as 'non-normative' (in that it does not adhere strictly to the syntactical, lexical, phonological or pragmatic norms of standard English variations), 'fluid and flexible' (i.e. rules and relative norms evolve over time and between encounters), 'co-constructive' (i.e. its local norms are co-developed on the fly by speakers) and 'listener-orientated' (i.e. speakers shape their utterances more carefully with their addressee's abilities in mind (Jenkins *et al*, 2011)). Above all, ELF has been found to be highly consensual and cooperative in nature (Firth, 2009; Jenkins, 2000; 2006; Pullin, 2013; Seidlhofer, 2011). In *not* being able to draw on shared cultural and linguistic resources, successful users of English as a Lingua Franca develop the ability to not only 'mediate between the world of origin and world of encountered difference' (Young & Sachdev, 2011: 83), but to occupy an emergent, intercultural space: or what has sometimes been referred to as a *third culture*.

In one of the earliest pieces of pragmatic research on English as a Lingua Franca, Firth (1996) identified an orientation towards consensus-building and a tendency towards preventative measures to protect against potential misunderstanding, rather than the more traditional repair or reformulation behaviours typically used by native speakers. Provided that a certain, basic threshold of understanding was achieved, ambiguities or linguistic infelicities (e.g. wrong grammar, wrong words, etc.) were seemingly otherwise ignored: a phenomenon Firth termed the *let-it-pass principle*. English as a Lingua Franca users, he found, were demonstrating a 'remarkable ability and willingness to tolerate anomalous usage and marked linguistic behaviour, even in the face of what appears ... to be usage that is at times acutely opaque (Firth, 1996: 247). Based on specific, 'quintessentially *local*[52] considerations' (Firth, 1996: 243), participants were choosing whether or not to attend to the anomalies in the unfolding interactions. Where the lack of understanding (in either direction) was deemed insignificant to the main aims of the communication, it was simply not acknowledged.

While there have been some contradictory results in more recent research suggesting that the let-it-pass principle may not be as prevalent as first

---

[52] 'Local', here, means pertaining to any specific encounter (as opposed to a particular place).

thought (e.g. Cogo & Dewey, 2006), it remains an interesting occurrence and in its reduced demands for perfect and fully coherent utterances, it is reminiscent of the 'low demand for coordination' thought by Heasman and Gillespie (2019) to be a feature of autistic sociality.

It might be worth signposting, here, that it is not my intention to suggest that being autistic entails belonging to an 'autistic culture'. Autistic (sub-)cultures do indeed exist, having developed in particular as autistic people have started finding each other online, and as autistic identities have begun to be embraced more openly. However, autistic people will also belong to any number of other wider and sub-cultures and there isn't one over-arching autistic culture we all belong to. What I'm trying to get to, by bringing in English as a Lingua Franca as a potential model of working, cross-dispositional communication is the *parallel* of how interaction can occur across the gaps of both cultures and of neurotypes. Alyssa Hillary (2020a: 95- 96), drawing on their experiences as an American autistic bilingual in China, perhaps exemplifies this more clearly:

> '*I was subtler in China than I am in the USA – I was trying to be culturally appropriate. However, the difference between how subtle I could be and how subtle I was expected to be remained larger in China than in the USA. Despite the larger gap, I got far more understanding in China, where the cultural difference was expected, than I did in the USA, where I'm simply expected to know better.*
>
> *[T]he double empathy problem was less of a problem for me in China, despite the greater difference in perspectives, because principles of cross-cultural communication were used over the idea that "I have a communication disorder, so this is my problem".*'

When Alyssa was interpreted as communicating across a cross-cultural gap, greater grace was given in the face of communication misalignments than when they were in their home country, communicating across a cross-neurotype gap. Consequentially, the double empathy problem was experienced as less of an issue and an impediment to mutual understanding when they were abroad, interacting as a 'foreigner', outside of their first culture. Alyssa's communicative self didn't inherently change, but the openness and willingness of their interlocutors to *go on* with them (as we saw in Chapter 5) did.

This, ultimately, brings us back around to the quotation from Jim Sinclair's (1993: 2) seminal *Don't Mourn For Us* speech that opened this chapter, but bears repeating:

> *'It takes more work to communicate with someone whose native language isn't the same as yours. And autism goes deeper than language and culture; autistic people are 'foreigners' in any society.'*

At an embodied, enactive level, autistic people are often *sensory strangers* (as we saw in Chapter 4) to those around them. Or, conversely, neurotypical people are sensory strangers to us, with whom it can be hard to attune, and who often refrain from extending the communicative grace that we have seen – in the case of English as a Lingua Franca – is absolutely possible to facilitate fruitful and mutually rewarding interactions.

In the next chapter (the final of our theory-building chapters) we'll look at how relevance theory might help us tie this all together and provide something of a linguistic explanation for what's happening when mutual understanding breaks down in cross-neurotype communication.

Chapter 8: But how's that relevant?

Throughout this book, we've looked at ideas about how cognising beings draw meaning from the world, both on their own and in consort with others. We've surveyed various historical and contemporary descriptions of autism stemming from the medical model and the neurodiversity paradigm. We've also explored various perspectives of autistic and cross-neurotype communication, including the double empathy problem and parallel concepts. All these disparate strands have been laid out ready to be woven together, in this chapter, where we'll attempt to explain what might be happening, in relevance theoretic terms, during double empathy problem communication breakdowns.

It was some time ago, however, that we last spoke about relevance theory (Chapter 3), so let's have a quick recap of its core tenets before we move on to look specifically at what relevance theory might have to say about cross-neurotype communication.

Relevance theory: a quick recap

Relevance theory (Sperber & Wilson, 1986; 1995) is a theory of both human cognition and communication. Its central goal is to answer the question: why is it that, against all the odds, communication usually *does* work, given that much of our intended meanings need to be derived *inferentially*?[53] Within the inferential model of human communication (as opposed to the code model), speakers are thought of as having communicative intentions (i.e. what they want to be communicated), that are expressed *ostensively* (i.e. spoken aloud so that their addressees may know that there is something the speaker wishes to convey). Because words and utterances can mean any number of things at any one time, listeners are required to infer the intended meaning (or the *implicature*). This is done, according to Sperber and Wilson, by identifying the most *relevant* meaning.

---

[53] If this is sounding a bit vague, skip back to the 'meaning and implied meaning' section in Chapter 3 for a refresh.

Because human cognition is geared towards a search for only the most relevant information in an otherwise overwhelming and unmanageable slew of data, we are able to safely assume that our communicative faculties have evolved so that every ostensive stimulus conveys what relevance theorists call a *presumption of its own optimal relevance*. In other words, we can assume that speakers won't purposefully drain an addressee's attention, and that any utterance will intuitively be crafted so as to be worth the addressee's precious processing effort, to the best of the speaker's abilities. As such, listeners should be able to identify the most relevant inference by completing the following heuristic:

> 'a. *Other things being equal, the greater the positive cognitive effects achieved by processing an input, the greater the relevance of the input to the individual at that time.*
>
> b. *Other things being equal, the greater the processing effort expended, the lower the relevance of the input to the individual at that time.*'
>
> (Wilson & Sperber, 2004: 609)

Here, *cognitive effects* refer to worthwhile differences to the addressee's representation of the world, including the strengthening, revision or abandonment of available assumptions. Relevance, then, is essentially the sweet spot between positive cognitive effects yielded, versus the processing effort required to get there.

Other key concepts from relevance theory that are pertinent to our thinking about cross-neurotype communication, are *cognitive environments*, *manifestness* and *mutual manifestness*. According to relevance theory, every individual has their own cognitive environment: the combination of all available (and potentially available) facts and assumptions in a given moment. These facts and assumptions that are within reach or potential reach (i.e. facts or assumptions that can be determined in a given moment, based on what is already known and an individual's cognitive abilities) are described as being *manifest*. When facts or assumptions are shared by two individuals and it is also manifest to those individuals that they are shared, these facts and assumptions are thought of as being part of a *mutual cognitive environment*. *Mutual manifestness*, finally, relates to the property of those shared facts and assumptions in a mutual cognitive environment.

It's worth noting that this doesn't mean that for something to be mutually manifest, an addressee and a speaker will need to have exactly the same contextual assumptions in the same moment. The addressee 'does not even have to have these assumptions stored in his memory. [They] must simply be able to construct them, either on the basis of what [they] can perceive in [their] immediate physical environment or on the basis of assumptions already stored in memory' (Sperber & Wilson 1995: 39).

Although a little complicated, the idea of mutual manifestness is important because it forms the basis of a listener's search for relevance. To the best of their abilities, speakers routinely (and intuitively) craft their utterances so as to be *optimally relevant* for their intended addressee. When an addressee is attempting to derive the intended *implicature* from the utterance a speaker has made, they will process the input, seeking out positive cognitive effects. The easier it is to process and the quicker it is to yield a positive cognitive effect, the more relevant the inference is, and therefore the most likely. Facts and assumptions that are more evidently mutually manifest will be easier to process than those that aren't. As communicators, we are constantly making preconscious evaluations about what is mutually manifest with our intended addressee and letting that shape our utterances.

All things being equal (until they aren't)

So why is this so important when we think about cross-neurotype interactions? Well, theories of communication and utterance interpretation – including relevance theory – are generally bounded by the caveat of 'all other things being equal' (as, indeed, we've seen above). What that's essentially saying is, 'so long as everything is as expected, then... [follow this procedure, etc.]'. This works perfectly fine when things *are* equal. However, what happens when they aren't?

Utterance interpretation, as with all aspects of cognition, takes a lot for granted in order to make quick decisions or inferences. We rely on 'fast and frugal'[54] (Gigerenzer & Todd, 1999) heuristics (i.e. rough mental shortcuts) to help us process large amounts of information and reach decisions faster, sometimes at the expense of accuracy. The heuristic used to determine relevance (outlined above), which in turn helps us select the correct inferences, works in just the same way. Calculations of common

---

54 Also sometimes referred to as being 'quick and dirty'.

ground (or, in relevance theoretic terms, what might be described as what is *mutually manifest*) are undertaken at lightning speed. The idea that we share common ground with our family members, loved ones, work colleagues, patients or service users with whom we appear to share contextual facts (i.e. we're sitting in the same waiting room, we live in the same house, we work on the same project or have the same role, we share an ethnicity, we live in the same part of the same country) is a reasonable thing to assume. And yet, when it comes to people of different neurotypes – particularly so for autistic and non-autistic people – the reality of what is actually shared is perhaps different to that which is immediately assumed. Let's look at that a little closer...

Living in (neuro)diverse worlds

Let's be frank. Autistic and non-autistic people experience the world differently. We know this. As embodied, enactive, cognising beings, humans make sense of the world around us using our sensory faculties as the starting point. In that way, we can also perhaps say that autistic people and non-autistic people live in different worlds. Reality, experienced through an autistic body with its divergent sensory, perceptual and interactive mechanisms, is coloured differently[55] to the reality experienced by non-autistic people. All of us (both neurotypical and neurodivergent) are individuals, with different bodies and different life experiences. Communicating with those who are different to ourselves – with those from other worlds – is something we do all the time. But there is, I think, something particularly unique about communication between those of differing neurotypes. The differences begin right at the very beginning of our sense-making, at the embodied, enactive, sensorial level. The Umwelten of autistic and non-autistic people, I suspect, diverge far more dramatically than those of any two, different neurotypical people.

As the now well-known expression goes, 'if you know one autistic person: you know one autistic person'. As we saw in Chapter 5, the category of 'autism' is characterised by heterogeneity. No two autistic people will experience exactly the same set of autistic traits, nor will they necessarily share similar Umwelten just because they're autistic. Precisely *because* of the atypicality of autistic sensory-perceptual experiences, the diversity of what is sensorily salient is likely to be even greater between autistic

---

55 It also tastes, feels, smells and sounds differently.

people. An autistic individual, say, who is highly attuned to micro-details in the auditory domain but hyposensitive to internal interoceptive cues will have a cognitive environment that is very different to that of another autistic individual who is hyper-alert to the sensation of touch and pressure and deeply engaged with minutiae in the visual domain but who struggles to differentiate voices from background noises.

Despite this, there is *something that it is like* to be autistic, that autistic people can recognise in themselves and in other autistic people. This expression 'something that is it like to be...' is used advisedly, as it references a train of thought sketched out by American philosopher Thomas Nagel (1974) while attempting to explain the phenomenon of consciousness. During his ponderings, he arrived at the following logical idea: any conscious being *must* have some subjective sense of *what it is like to be itself*. For his exemplar, he wanted to think about the phenomenal experience of being a bat. And yet he hit a stumbling block. A bat uses sonar – a sense that humans do not possess – as its principal means of interpreting and navigating the world. If we were to try to imagine the subjective experience (or, the Umwelt) of a bat, we would only ever achieve a mediocre facsimile as we lack the embodied, enacting sensory faculties to accurately represent a bat's *way of being* in the world. We can only get so far in imagining a world sparkling in echolocative salience when we have never known what it is to experience echolocation. We can perhaps imagine what it's like to hang upside-down by our feet in a cave a little easier, but our imaginings would be troubled by our knowledge of how gravity works on our bodies and how it feels to have a sudden rush of blood to the head. In essence: we cannot know what it is like to be a bat.

Thinking about this shared *something that it is like to be* autistic, a handful of autistic autism theorists (including Robert Chapman (2019) and Nick Chown, (2012)) have drawn on the work of early 20th-century philosopher and linguist Ludwig Wittgenstein[56] and his notion of *forms of life*. Very broadly, from a Wittgensteinian perspective, *forms of life* refer to the groupings of individuals who share representational forms (i.e. mental concepts of the world around them). A form of life shared by a set of individuals encompasses not only the language they use to communicate and their cultural practices and values, but also the concepts

---

[56] Wittgenstein was also a source of inspiration for linguist Paul Grice, whose maxims (see Chapter 3) in turn inspired Deidre Wilson and Dan Sperber's relevance theory.

that the world (as they experience it) is organised into. In this sense, then, members of a form of life might be thought of as sharing similar Umwelten.

Chapman (2019) makes the argument that the double empathy problem is akin to a mutual *aspect-blindness* (drawing on further Wittgensteinian terminology), where parties have 'some level of understanding but nonetheless miss certain aspects' (2019a: 429). Given the different attunements to and experiences of the world(s) around them – both on account of divergent sensory-perceptual-cognitive faculties and the experience of growing up as either a neuro-majority or neurominority – autistic and non-autistic people will ultimately belong to different forms of life. As such, each will struggle with a degree of aspect-blindness when communicating with someone from a different form of life. As Wittgenstein himself put it, just like with Nagel's bats: 'if a lion could speak, we would not understand him' (1968: 223e).

In a not dissimilar vein to the forms of life idea, Elizabeth Fein – a psychological anthropologist who spent several years conducting ethnographic research around the autism diagnostic process and the experiences of autistic adolescents transitioning into adulthood in the US – arrived at a conceptualisation of autism as a distinct *mode of engagement* with the world:

> 'What is this thing that I study, that I chase after, that I dance around, and try in fleeting moments to dance with? The thing I study is more like color than like color-blindness—it's a thing that happens between sensing bodies and sensuous worlds, in all the particularity of each. I have come to think of the thing I seek out as a mode of engagement with the stuff of the world—a way of being with one's surroundings…'
>
> (Fein, 2018: 130)

I find this framing particularly useful because it reminds us of the sensorial basis of the embodied, enacted differences between autistic and non-autistic people. Yet all of the above, really, are simply different ways of speaking to the same fact: that autistic people and non-autistic people experience differently salient worlds. Grounded in embodied, phenomenological difference, the worlds of autistic and non-autistic people are experienced differently. As such, the representations and concepts that autistic and non-autistic people hold may be tweaked in different directions, and will certainly be organised differently in the mind. Things that seem obvious to autistic people will not always be so for non-autistic people, and vice versa.

Differences in salience in cross-neurotype encounters

And here is where relevance theory has its moment to shine. According to relevance theory we, as speakers, craft utterances to be as *optimally relevant* for our addressee as we can (to the best of our abilities at any time). We do so by evaluating (in micro-second timescales) what is mutually manifest between ourselves and our addressee. As listeners, we, in turn, follow a relevance-seeking heuristic: weighing up the amount of positive cognitive effects gained versus the effort required to determine them. Yet, if concepts are organised in our minds in significantly different orders, or are more or less salient, these helpful heuristics start to become less helpful.

A potentially useful way to think about this is by imagining the different ways that any two individuals might interpret any one thing, in the case of *Figure 3*, a piece of impressionistic artwork in a gallery:

Figure 3: Two individuals interpreting an image differently.

One person might look at the artwork on the wall and be reminded of mountains. It might bring to mind the recollection of a pleasant holiday, years before, when they took a trip in a hot air balloon and first realised how small we are as humans. Another might instead notice the bold geometric shapes, or think about it in terms of artistic composition, noticing the colours and the harshness of the lines. Although there are often intended effects from a piece of art, these tend to be a bit looser (e.g. for the viewer to be moved, or to be pleased or for the work to reference a certain style) and artistic works often carry an array of weaker, intended potential effects (see Wharton & Kolaiti, 2024). In other words, it is expected that different viewers will draw different meanings and feelings.

In the case of our two gallery-goers, the different interpretations of the piece on the wall arise due to differences in what is most salient to them at the time of standing before the artwork. This will be affected by any number of personal and contextual factors – e.g. what they each learned in school, what they heard on the radio that morning, how sluggish they feel, how well-hydrated they are… When it comes to the interpretation of artwork, a range of inferences are to be expected. However, with most spoken (or: *ostensive-inferential*) communication, there is usually a clearly determined addressee (or audience of addressees) and a clear sense of intended meaning. Speakers have something they wish to communicate. And because, as we've seen in earlier chapters, meaning is not a standardised thing and needs to be derived via inference, listeners are tasked with determining the correct implicature.

All things being equal, we do this by following a relevance-seeking heuristic. We test out the various potential implicatures (intended meanings) until we hit a goldmine of positive cognitive effects (i.e. we gain some new contextual information, or we strengthen or disavow existing assumptions, etc.). The longer we spend testing out different interpretations, the more cognitive effort we're expending and so (according to the heuristic) the less relevant (and therefore the less likely) the interpretation is. Let's think about this in the context of cross-neurotype encounters.

We know, now, that genes, the brain, cognition and our environment all interact multi-directionally throughout an individual's development (Karmiloff-Smith, 2006; 2009). Neural connectivity, as well as gene expression, is shaped and changed across an individual's lifespan in response to the bodily and external environments an individual finds themself in. In other words, the way we perceive the world shapes how we pay attention to it, which in turn shapes what we perceive. Across a lifespan, we develop unique trajectories of enacting our worlds.

We also know that autism is characterised by sensory-perceptual and attentional differences that are present from birth. The divergent sensory experience of autistic people will have a bearing not only on how they experience their environment in any given moment, but also on how they think about and understand the world around them. For all of us, sensory representations form the building blocks for higher-order perceptual and cognitive representations (Baum *et al*, 2015), which in turn feed into what we notice and pay attention to. Add this to the atypical, often monotropic attentional styles of autistic people and you start to create, across development, cognitive environments that are organised quite differently to those of non-autistic people, populated by potentially quite different representations and concepts.

Crucially, degrees of salience of any given concept, representation or assumption for autistic and non-autistic people may vary widely. As such, which facts and assumptions are manifest at any given time, and which representations are most accessible, may not be in any way similar for autistic and non-autistic people, even if they appear to have lots in common. The degree of cognitive effort required to generate certain cognitive effects will also, therefore, be different. And here, I think, is where the double empathy problem has its basis. The relevance-seeking recipe followed will be the same, but the values will be different. I might craft my utterance perfectly, to the best of my abilities, to be optimally relevant to you, my addressee, based on what I believe to be mutually manifest. I judge that my intended implicature will be uncostly (in terms of cognitive effort) for you to determine, based on what I believe we both know we're both capable of knowing at that moment (i.e. what is mutually manifest). But if, for some reason, your cognitive environment is different to my expectation, you may well find it takes a lot more effort for you to arrive at my intended implicature. There may be, instead, an alternative implicature that comes to you more readily, requiring less effort. Believing that I have crafted my utterance to be optimally relevant, and following the relevance-seeking heuristic, you'll stop searching for meaning once you reach that first (although incorrect) implicature. In such an instance, communication breaks down. To borrow the title of Damian Milton's (2017) collected essays on the double empathy problem, it was all down to a *mismatch of salience*.

Taking it for granted

In the last chapter, we made a brief sojourn around English as a Lingua Franca and the unique way it is used and developed in the moment between speakers for whom English is not their first language[57]. Here, we saw how two speakers with sometimes very little in common, and limited shared linguistic resources, can and do achieve sophisticated mutual understanding. A crucial ingredient, I believe, in these interactions is the fact that *it is mutually manifest that little is mutually manifest*. In other words, both speakers enter into these interactions alert to the fact that they do not know what the other might know or be able to know. On the simplest level, even where speakers may share a physical environment (e.g. be sat in the same boardroom) and come from similar cultures, it takes time to attune their ear to another English as a Lingua Franca user's use of the language, infelicities and all.

As with interactions mediated by English as a Lingua Franca, in cross-neurotype encounters, we have two speakers with potentially very differently organised cognitive environments, made up of differently salient representations. However, unlike in English as a Lingua Franca interactions, this difference is often *not* mutually manifest. Particularly so when cross-neurotype interactions happen between speakers from a shared background or with a lot of contextual facts and assumptions apparently in common, a lot is taken for granted as being shared (or as being mutually manifest). In English as Lingua Franca interactions, differences in salience are easier to explain. It seems reasonable to assume that someone from another culture, with a different language background, might see things differently from us. But someone we share our daily life with? Someone we go to school with? Someone who lives next door? The idea that they might perceive the world so dramatically differently is harder to imagine.

This may also go some way towards explaining why it is that autistic in-group interactions seem to go smoothly, despite the myriad of different potential ways of being and presenting as autistic. While autistic individuals' cognitive environments and communicative habits may vary distinctly, it may be that autistic people recognise each other as similarly outside of local (neurotypical) norms. Autistic people are likely to have a better intuitive understanding of how it might be to

---

[57] A more accurate definition would in fact be: 'any use of English among speakers of different first languages for whom English is the communicative medium of choice, and often the only option' (Seidlhofer, 2011: 7).

experience and understand the world differently (as this is a fact they will have been confronted with since infancy) and, as such, factor this in when evaluating another's cognitive environment. In other words, when two autistic people interact – even those who are strangers, and with diverging maps of salience – it may be that it is more automatically mutually manifest (as it is in English as a Lingua Franca interactions) that fewer facts and assumptions are shared. As such (and in the same way as English as a Lingua Franca interactions) a *generosity of interpretation* may be triggered; characterised, perhaps, by a broader search for potential, relevant interpretations. In other words, fewer assumptions about mutual manifestness will be made and expectations for references to things outside of a shared cognitive repertoire will be increased. Autistic speakers may be more prepared and more willing to make extra efforts in the search for relevance or (in English as a Lingua Franca researcher Frith's terms) to simply *let it pass*.

A brief note on existing ideas from relevance theory about autism

This isn't the first time that relevance theory has been used when thinking about autistic or cross-neurotype communication, although previous efforts haven't been as neurodiversity-affirming. A number of papers have been published using relevance theory as a means of exploring autistic 'pragmatic impairment' (e.g Happé, 1991; 1993; 1995; Leinonen & Kerbel, 1999; Leinonen & Ryder, 2008; Loukusa *et al*, 2007; Papp, 2006; Wearing, 2010). However, to be fair to relevance theorists, because intention recognition is such a fundamental aspect of the account of utterance interpretation, many only really knew about autism as a kind of test case for communication involving (supposed) impaired theory of mind abilities.

One of the more interesting examples of how relevance theorists have thought about autistic communication might be comments by Dan Sperger, co-originator of relevance theory, in an online discussion in 2004 (in Wharton, 2014: 479). Sperber felt sure that autistic people, just like neurotypicals, must be processing information according to the same principles of relevance. The cause of these common breakdowns in (mutual) understanding, he mused, might be something to do with a paucity of input:

> *'[Autistic people] are using the relevance-theoretic comprehension procedure and following a path of least effort, but on the basis of impoverished input caused by their inability to interpret natural pragmatic clues such as gaze direction, pointing, facial expressions, etc.'*
>
> (Sperber, 2004, in an online discussion, in Wharton 2014: 479).

The positive, here, is that this assertion affords autistic people a suite of cognitive abilities (including a relevance-seeking heuristic) that function in a very human way, against the backdrop of historically dehumanising autism research. However, it takes as its starting point the idea that autistic people are inherently pragmatically impaired; something we now know to be untrue. There is also an important difference between (a) struggling to draw correct inferences from an impoverished input and (b) working with an adequately rich input, but according to differently organised salience. This difference is important because the latter means that there is scope to negotiate understanding, if both parties involved are willing to expend extra efforts...

Making the effort

When we communicate between different forms of life, we are talking between worlds. If we do it right, we build a new, third world: one that is shared and populated by objects of both the known and the 'other' world, sometimes blended together and made anew. In English as Lingua Franca interactions, this is called a *third culture* (Young & Sachdev, 2011). In relevance-theoretic terms, you might say that we're building new (and larger) mutual cognitive environments. It is more than translation: it is transformational. In that way, it is magic.

To move into a third space takes energy. It requires both effort – in the form of cognitive efforts, as measured in the relevance-seeing heuristic – and awareness of the need to do so. As it is so often the neuro-minoritised person who first suffers from the mismatch of realities, it tends to fall to them to take on the extra work of accommodating the perspective from another form of life. Traditional perspectives on autism that view autistic people as 'impaired' communicators place the burden on autistic people to mask or camouflage their natural behaviours in order to perform communicatively as neurotypicals do (see Pearson & Rose, 2023).

In practical terms, young autistic people are often subjected to Applied Behavioural Analysis (ABA), a form of behavioural training that many of those who have experienced it describe as traumatising and unethical (Anderson, 2023).

For the autistic individual whose way of being is at odds with that of the neuro-majority, there is a greater imperative to bridge the gap: to not be left misunderstood, to not be overlooked, to be heard. This imperative – as we'll see in the following chapter – is no trivial matter. For many, our lives and well-being depend upon it.

Section 4
Divergent minds and diverse societies

Chapter 9: The importance of getting it right

Trigger warning: death by suicide

In June 2023, Donald Gray Triplett III died at the grand age of 89, at his home in Mississippi. Those of you with eagle eyes may recognise the name *Donald T.* from Chapter 5, where he was introduced as Leo Kanner's first ever autistic patient, diagnosed in the 1930s. Despite receiving a pathologising diagnosis and being described in – at times – quite dehumanising terms, obituaries written after his death paint a portrait of a man who 'had found a niche' (Mandy, 2023: 1854) and lived a seemingly happy and fulfilling life.

This, for me, feels like such a delicious coup: that Mr Triplett was able to go on and live in ways that (as far as we can tell) worked well for him. It also probably, as autism researcher Will Mandy has observed, reflects the working out of a 'good fit between, on the one hand, his individual characteristics, needs and motivations and, on the other, the demands and opportunities provided by his environment' (*Ibid*). In that way, then, Mr Triplett may have ultimately been luckier than many of his fellow autistic people. He found himself work that he was able to thrive in, developed a hobby (golfing) that he was able to practice almost every day, and found love and acceptance in his local community, where people would often join him as he sat outside his favourite café. For many autistic people, however, it is all too often the case that they struggle to find their niche in a world designed for, and populated in the majority by, non-autistic people.

Loneliness and social isolation

In the same year, some colleagues and I published the findings from some research we had done into autistic people's experiences of loneliness (in Quadt *et al*, 2023). Loneliness is a 'universal affliction' (McGraw, 1995: 43) that almost all people will experience at some point in their lives. For many, it is a more serious, enduring and distressing state. Often operationalised as the 'discrepancy between one's desired and achieved levels of social relations' (Perlman & Peplau, 1981: 32), we now know that loneliness is a risk factor for various health problems and increased mortality rates (e.g. Holt-Lunstad, Smith, and Layton, 2010; Valtorta, 2016; Wong et al, 2017). Autistic people are especially prone to loneliness and social isolation (National Autistic Society, 2018) and for autistic people, loneliness is additionally associated with increased depression and anxiety (Mazurek, 2014) and self-injurious behaviours (Hedley et al, 2018).

My colleagues and I combined two separate smaller studies: both offshoots of larger projects. Some of our data came from a set of 209 questionnaires completed by autistic and non-autistic people that measured their levels of loneliness, anxiety, depression and sensory differences. In addition to the usual, standardised questions, we added an extra dimension: asking participants to answer, 'How much does this upset you?' following each factor on the loneliness questionnaire[58]. The other half of our data was comprised of the things that autistic people had said about their experiences of loneliness during the pilot community engagement project (described in Chapter 6) that had been the source of the linguistic data for my doctoral research. Together, we compared our findings.

Above all, what stood out was the extent to which autistic people reported being distressed by their experiences of loneliness. In the first set of data, as well as rating themselves more highly than their non-autistic peers on the loneliness questionnaire, autistic respondents also gave higher ratings for the 'how much does this upset you?' questions. In the second set, autistic participants described a sometimes-intense pain of feeling lonely and socially isolated. In summary, not only were autistic people more likely to experience loneliness than non-autistic people, but they were also more likely to be distressed by it. This was borne out in the things autistic people said about their loneliness in the second dataset:

Peter[59]: Cos I feel, you know, say I'm in a group of people and they're all chatting away ... cos I'm not on, I'm not on their level [...] I feel lonely even though I'm in that, that group: I feel lonely just sitting there.

---

58 So, for each question on the loneliness questionnaire (e.g. 'I lack companionship'), participants would also answer 'how much does this upset you?'.
59 Names have been changed for anonymity.

Sarah: I'm trying to reach out, I'm trying to find my people, but it's not – as you say – it's not connecting deeply within me; it all still feels a bit hopeless and superficial.

Molly: I want to, like, actually, like, make a connection with someone ... it's having people to actually talk, like talk openly to.
(Quadt et al, 2023: 11)

While participants *did* also describe a need for time to themselves to recover from social overwhelm, they often expressed a deep desire for meaningful connections with other people, which they found hard to find. Reasons given for this included difficulty in connecting with non-autistic people who seemed not to understand them, and the struggle to find people with similar (sometimes intense) interests. In addition to these, participants also spoke about a general feeling of being misunderstood and unaccepted by society as a whole: something that elsewhere has been described as ethical loneliness.

Ethical loneliness

The term *loneliness* can refer to a range of experiences, including some that go beyond the oft-cited definition of loneliness as the gap between the number and kind of social relations that one has, and that one wants (Perlman & Peplau, 1981). For example, in a cross-sectional, qualitative study investigating older people's loneliness in Hong Kong, Wong *et al* (2017) discovered that a significant factor influencing the extent to which older people felt lonely was a sense of increased alienation from society as a whole. As they gradually entered their older years, Hong-Kongese elders were seemingly experiencing a sequence of alienating events: the insufficiency of a national care system unfit to properly meet their needs; a growing distance between themselves and the rest of society; and a disintegration of their previous identity within society. Crucially, they reported feeling that their voices were not listened to and that, as a result, their lives felt insignificant. In sum, the researchers concluded, they were experiencing what might be called *ethical loneliness*.

The term was first coined by philosopher Jill Stauffer (2015) to describe the experience of being both abandoned by humanity and not having the wrongdoings against you acknowledged. According to Stauffer:

> 'Ethical loneliness is the isolation one feels when one, as a violated person or as a member of a persecuted group, has been abandoned by humanity, or by those who have power over one's life possibilities. It is a condition undergone by persons who have been unjustly treated and dehumanised by human beings and political structures, who emerge from that injustice only to find that the surrounding world will not listen to or cannot properly hear their testimony – their claims about what they suffered and about what is now owed to them – on their own terms.'
>
> (Stauffer, 2015: 1)

While Stauffer's work was primarily concerned with political injustices and extreme human rights violations such as torture, it seems particularly pertinent when thinking about loneliness and autism. Not being able to make yourself understood and not being able to connect in a satisfying way with fellow humans, can create a deep sense of alienation. Not having this pain acknowledged can compound the feeling of dehumanisation. This was a sentiment that was echoed in many of the conversations about loneliness held by our autistic participants, including Peter[60], an autistic man in his 50s with an additional learning disability:

> '...with me having, erm, having, erm, autism, and learning disabilities, I mean I understand a bit more about it today than I did do, but when I wasn't getting the support I felt very lonely... You know, cos, er, you know, you know I didn't have any connection... I was crying out for that support.'
>
> '...and when you phone it [a helpline] no one ever answers. I mean, I think someone will answer it eventually but from my experience no one's ever answered it. I've never actually spoken to a person on the other end of the line on this, what-whatever number it was... You know, if people are crying out for help because of how they feel and there's no help then of course they're going to feel lonely or, you know, get into a state...'
>
> (Quadt et al, 2023: 12)

---

60 Again, not his real name.

In his descriptions of support phonelines not answering his calls, Peter is essentially telling us how his 'cries for help' weren't being heard. That, according to Stauffer (2015: 5), is a key part of ethical loneliness that is 'more profound than simple isolation'.

Anomie and normlessness

In 2020 – ironically, just before vast swathes of the global population entered into a series of COVID-19 'lockdowns' – Jeste, Lee and Cacioppo published a psychiatry journal opinion piece about loneliness and the impact it was having on our modern lives. In it, they described loneliness as a 'hard to detect and lethal behavioural toxin' (2020: 1), and argued that it was a significant contributing factor in the growing suicide and opiate epidemics, particularly in the US. Speculating on the cause of this 'loneliness epidemic', they suggest an 'underlying thread of social anomie and disconnection' (Jeste *et al*, 2020).

The term *anomie* was originally coined by sociologist Durkheim (1897) in his monograph about the growing incidence rate of suicide in newly industrialised France (and Europe). Capitalism was beginning to boom, bringing both wealth potential and an erosion of previously long-established social norms, seeing the influence of religion and family on individual choices gradually weaken. Durkheim was witnessing a sharp increase in general despair around him that was exemplified, most tellingly, in a surge in the number of suicides. Durkheim theorised anomie to be a condition that was experienced during moments of social or political change, either on an individual level (i.e. when suddenly coming into a life-changing sum of money, or conversely, losing it and finding oneself in a new echelon of society) or a national one (such as during times of war). In such moments, he thought that individuals would find themselves in a position where the norms and values they had previously held dear were no longer reflected in the society around them, engendering a profound sense of disconnection.

While the meaning of anomie has broadened to include a sense of societal normlessness, or a 'condition [of the social system] in which the norms have lost their regulatory power' (Seeman, 1975: 102), it is perhaps also helpful to think of anomie not only as a lack, but as a *mismatch* of norms. Thinking about anomie in this way may help draw out the connection between being autistic and experiencing ethical loneliness. For example, one very common thread among self-descriptions of being autistic is the sense of feeling 'alien' or 'other'. Autistic people often describe feeling outside of the culture – or the set of norms – they've grown up around, as exemplified by autistic scholars Jackson-Perry, Bertilsdotter-Rosqvist, Annable and Kourti (2020) in their reflections on experiencing social life as a *sensory stranger*:

> 'I often feel that everyone else has the same cultural background [to start from] and I don't. And that makes me feel broken, out of place, less, someone who cannot be accounted for, included or accommodated for.
>
> 'It's frustrating when only one person in the world speaks your language and everybody else can only communicate with you through your second, third, fourth etc. language but not your mother tongue.'
> (Jackson-Perry *et al*, 2020: 128/130)

This sense of alienation is perhaps unsurprising, given the extent to which autistic people are routinely 'othered' in both macro- and micro-social ways. Recall, for example, how (in Chapter 6) research by Sasson *et al* (2017) identified how non-autistic people tend to form preconscious, negative judgements about autistic individuals within the first few seconds of meeting them. Autistic people, too, are more likely than non-autistic people to suffer abuse of some form (e.g. Bargiela *et al*, 2016; Haruvi-Lamdan *et al*, 2020; Stalker & McArthur, 2012; Sullivan & Knutson, 2000; Weiss & Fardella, 2018), including interpersonal victimisation and violence (Pearson *et al*, 2022; Pearson *et al*, 2023). At the wider societal level, environments aren't designed with autistic people's needs in mind (Manning *et al*, 2023), creating a culture of exclusion: as is often borne out to the extreme in educational settings (see Moyse, 2021). Even when autistic people aren't facing direct discrimination or victimisation, they still exist at a disadvantage due to the fact that the societal norms and values around them are often uncomfortably mismatched with their own. If you don't have similar thought processes to those around you, if you can't find anyone to share your interests, if the norms and values of the people around you seem alien, it is hard to feel that you belong.

In discussing what it might take to redress the harms done by society to those whose humanity has been overlooked, or intentionally violated, Stauffer suggests the following:

> 'A survivor will need broad social support that functions as a promise that, though she was once abandoned by humanity, that will not be allowed to happen again. That is an act of world building, which is a cooperative enterprise, not a solitary endeavour.'
>
> (Stauffer, 2015: 7)

It is the promise of meaningful engagement with others, and the promise that previously ignored voices will now be heard, that is most important, according to Stauffer, for establishing trust in a world rife with systemic oppression. This healing, restorative process, involving radical conceptual change about who matters, who is safe, and who belongs in the world following an instance or period of profound disconnection from it, she termed *world-building*. World-building cannot be done alone. There must be the hand of another reaching out towards our own outstretched palm. There must be another to truly hear us and to bear witness. Or, as Stauffer (2015: 19) put it, '*my sovereignty depends*'.

And yet, many autistic people do not have the luxury of experiencing the restorative act of *world-building*. Instead, many face micro-aggressions of ethical loneliness over and over (and over) again across a lifetime. Like Peter, whose calls for help were ultimately left unanswered, many autistic people don't have access to rich and supportive community networks. This, it is important to emphasise, is not because of some inherent autistic inability to connect with others. It is, instead, due to the impoverished opportunities to participate in a shared *form of life* (where non-autistic people are the neuro-majority) and because of the limited accessibility of public spaces and services where shared life takes place.

This sense (and the reality) of being abandoned by society has a great bearing on autistic people's lives. While writing this book I lost a very dear autistic friend of mine, who died by suicide. Words cannot really do justice to the sorrow I felt, nor any of the many other feelings that rise up with grief: guilt, denial, terror... But as life-changingly tragic as it was, I don't think I can say that it was a huge surprise. Nor, awfully, was she the first autistic person in my circle to die this way. As an autism researcher, I am all too familiar with the statistics. For autistic adults, the suicide rate is nine times that of non-autistic adults (Hirvikoski *et al*, 2016) and studies involving autistic children have found that 11% have suicidal ideation (Mayes *et al*, 2013). And the group most likely to die by suicide? Autistic women and those assigned female at birth who do not have additional learning disabilities (Hirvikoski et al, 2016).

I don't think it's quite so simple to say that my friend died directly due to ethical loneliness, but I do believe that she suffered from the lack of a safety net, from patchy and absent support systems hollowed out by government austerity measures, and from an enduring sense that she couldn't find her niche of safety and acceptance. For another (also autistic) friend, who also died by suicide the year before, I would say the story is very similar, if exacerbated at the end by terminally traumatising interactions with ineffectual services, unaware of how to communicate with autistic people in distress.

When understanding breaks down, when communication doesn't work, we cannot thrive. A lifetime of othering interactions takes its toll.

Societal and environmental alienation and exclusion

One further, interesting, and somewhat surprising finding from our loneliness research, was the direct link we found between people's sensory processing and their tendency to experience loneliness[61]. Higher self-ratings of sensory processing differences (and sensory sensitivities) were connected to increased loneliness and poorer mental health: in both autistic and non-autistic adults. However, this association was especially strong for our autistic participants – understandable, perhaps, given that autistic people are known to experience sensory processing differences (as we saw in Chapter 4).

Among the recorded conversations about loneliness, we also noted how many autistic people spoke about the practical barriers they face to finding and building social connections. Some, for example, described the financial barriers they encountered when wanting to attend clubs or courses, or social spaces like pubs. One factor at play here is the extant 'cost-of-living crisis' in the UK and the fact that the city where the research took place is particularly afflicted. However, it is also fair to say that both disabled people in general in the UK, and specifically autistic people, are at an increased risk of experiencing financial hardship due to barriers to accessing employment and benefits (Grant et al, 2023). Yet of the

---

61 See Quadt et al (2023) for further detail.

practical barriers described, one of the most significant was the difficulty of navigating sensorily overwhelming urban environments and the ways in which this inhibited our autistic participants from connecting with others.

As Manning and colleagues, myself included, (2023) have argued, while there is a slowly growing body of research investigating the sensory processing differences of autistic people, there have been grievously few projects looking at the ways in which aversive sensory environments tax autistic people's sensory processing, nor are there funding initiatives to develop sensory-friendly urban infrastructure. This is despite the fact that autistic people speak up at every given opportunity about the access barriers and sensory distress they experience in many public spaces.

Take, for example, healthcare provision in the UK[62]. As was touched on above, autistic people are more susceptible not only to loneliness and mental health issues like anxiety (Buck *et al*, 2014) and depression (Uljarević *et al*, 2020), but also serious physical medical conditions, including things like hypertension and diabetes (Doherty *et al*, 2022). In addition, some research has pointed to autistic people being more likely to die (than non-autistic people) from almost all medical conditions (Hirvikoski *et al*, 2016). Yes, you read that correctly. All medical conditions. And, finally, average autistic lifespans appear to be somewhere between 16 and 30 years shorter than matched non-autistic peers (Doherty *et al*, 2022; Hirvikoski *et al*, 2016).

Despite all this, healthcare provision in the UK remains fraught with manifold barriers for autistic people when it comes to accessing services, further compounding the health gap they experience (Doherty *et al*, 2022). Notably, communication difficulties with healthcare staff are frequently reported as one of the most challenging barriers to accessing appropriate care (Raymaker *et al*, 2017; Mason *et al*, 2019; Doherty *et al*, 2022). However, many other barriers relate to the unfavourable sensory environments of medical premises. In some cases, these act as a deterrent against autistic patients attending in the first place (Williams *et al*, 2022), having a knock-on effect on the underdiagnosis of life-threatening illness. In other instances, hostile sensory environments can exacerbate conditions

---

62 A lot of the data in this chapter relates to the experience of autistic people in the UK, as that is where I've grown up and had lived experience of being an autistic person. It's also where I've conducted my own research. In other words, it's the context I am most familiar with and able to speak to. While it may seem intuitive that this is a universal issue for autistic people all around the world, more research and research funding is absolutely needed to identify the culturally specific needs of autistic people in different national contexts.

such as in the case of autistic children and young people spending extended periods of time on long-stay inpatient mental health wards where the sensory-induced distress behaviours often trigger a cycle of progressing through increasingly restrictive (and sensory-unfriendly) settings (see Williams *et al*, 2023).

Similar themes also came up in another piece of research I was involved in (Blood *et al*, 2023; Blood *et al*, in prep.), commissioned by one local council authority to investigate why neurodivergent people seemed to be over-represented among those seeking support out of homelessness. We spoke with a number of neurodivergent people living in supported accommodation with experience of homelessness. Some described difficulties they had experienced with the sensory environments of shared hostel accommodation: a factor which might drive neurodivergent people with sensory processing differences towards taking their chances living on the street. One person I interviewed was living in supported accommodation next to a nightclub. As I was leaving, he asked me if there was any way I could help with the loud music coming from the nightclub next door – that had already begun during the course of the interview in the early evening – as it kept him up every night and was preventing him from sleeping. He'd asked staff at the supported accommodation but his requests had been left unanswered...

On not hearing or not listening to autistic people

In a different study, this one investigating the autistic sensory experiences of public spaces, MacLennan *et al* (2023: 411) found that 'supermarkets, eateries ... highstreets and city/town centres, public transport, healthcare settings (i.e., doctor's surgeries and hospitals), and retail shops and shopping centres' were all described as being disabling sensory environments. These kinds of public spaces were often experienced as overwhelming, with inescapable multi-sensory inputs that effectively prevented autistic people from showing up. Notably, of the six key themes the authors identified to describe factors that comprise the *big spider web of things* (to borrow the paper's title) that make public spaces disabling, two related to communication.

While the other four (sensoryscape, space, predictability and recovery) related to aspects of the built environment (e.g. sensory burden, busy and crowded, lack of information, no space to escape), the remaining two involved the influence of other people. For example, in the *understanding* theme, autistic participants spoke about the misunderstandings and negative judgements they had experienced around their challenges with intense sensory environments, often making them feel misunderstood or stigmatised. In the *adjustments* theme, non-autistic people's inflexibility around communication was reported as a common barrier:

'Several autistic adults described how there was an expectation in public places to use spoken language to communicate, which could be challenging and anxiety provoking to navigate. Some individuals described how feeling overwhelmed by the sensory environment impacted their ability to use speech to express themselves. In addition, many autistic adults described how public places that do not accommodate different communication needs and preferences can be disabling and impact individuals accessing goods and services.'

(Maclennan *et al*, 2023: 418)

The idea that non-autistic people don't (or aren't willing to) understand autistic people's sensory distress is reflected elsewhere, including in a study by Parmer and colleagues (2021) on autistic people's visual sensory experiences in the context of their daily lives. Here, participants similarly described feeling anxious about finding themselves in situations where they would need to try to explain their sensory challenges.

Talking about sensory distress and inhospitable sensory environments may, at first glance, seem something of a tangent in a book about cross-neurotype communication, but its inclusion is purposeful. Firstly, being overwhelmed by intense sensory input may make it harder for an autistic person to communicate (or think, or hold back the tide of a meltdown) in any given moment. And secondly, having sensory experiences of the world that diverge deeply from those of the person you're talking to may make your mutual cognitive environment smaller, and mutual manifestness less easy to predict. But more than that, the studies and examples above are most relevant because they demonstrate the ways in which society systematically fails to listen to autistic people. Our social and societal worlds are organised without autistic people's needs in mind and our towns and cities are layer upon layer of environments that don't often accommodate autistic body-minds or autistic forms of life. And then, when autistic people express their distress, or their sense of alienation... they are ignored.

If we follow Stauffer's advice, then reparative acts of *world-building* are required: borne from the act of 'hearing well' (2015: 76). And this must be led by non-autistic people. It must be the non-autistic people in positions of privilege or power who lead the listening and who allow themselves to be moved by autistic people's storying of themselves. Non-autistic people need to *believe* autistic people, and to do that they need to allow the possibility of a world (or a perceptual experience of it) that is different from their own. They need to consider other forms of life – something we perhaps all need to do now more than ever, the growing precarity of life on Earth and the imperative to live more in harmony with our non-human neighbours (Tamas, 2020).

If there is a take-away message, from this chapter, it is that communication matters; being heard matters; and being understood matters. In the next chapter, we'll look in closer detail at how some autistic people experience both additional marginalisation and poorer representation in public perceptions of what it means to be autistic.

***

```
The insects are dropping out of the skies. The
hymenoptera are pulling off a world-class magic trick
and disappearing behind their own veils. 'Colony
Collapse Disorder' on a mass scale. I read it in the
news this morning (a sign of 'pervasive and ongoing
environmental damage', it said) but it's something
I've known for years. I'd seen it in the colonies of
my companions and it had rustled through networks of
beekeepers across the country, word-of-mouth, like
wildfire. The uncertainty. The powerlessness of facing
an unknown assailant.

In ten years I'd not lost a colony, and these girls
I'd brought with me not so long ago I'd had with me
since the very beginning, hardy, half wild, now. I'd
```

brought them here at night, accompanied by friends bribed by beer and the promise of a unique evening. Sat, back soft against the beehive, head arced upwards so that my skull connected with its wooden frame, conducting the hum through to my middle ear. Stillness in motion, velvet blackness the unlit back of the transit van. A prayer whispered along the motorway, honey-breathed and hive-eyed. Stars out, arriving late. Wet grass and heavy hefting, whispered instructions and hushed grunts. The instant gentle hum, the propolis scent spilling out into the night, us standing back, reverent.

But as the weeks had progressed and first, snowdrops then, trumpet-vined bindweed had replaced the white of the frost with their own white flags, the bees did not quite seem to believe that it was safe to come out. Tentative at the entrance, small in number.

Then one sundown, ambling over to the hive, backlit by a champagne and salmon sky, I saw that the bee at the entrance looked odd. Dropping into a crouch, keeping a respectful distance, I peered closer. Not a bee, but a yellow-jacket wasp, robbing the hive.

The bees were gone.

Chapter 10: The importance of intersectional thinking

Communication never happens between just two isolated individuals. There is always a social context, shaping not just what we say and how we say it, but also – to an extent – what we think (and want to communicate) in the first place. In relevance-theoretic terms, social and environmental context shapes the mutual cognitive environment shared by any two communicators, and what is (and isn't) mutually manifest.

We've spent the majority of this book talking about 'autistic people', primarily in contrast and in relation to 'non-autistic' people. But in doing so, the illusion has perhaps been created that there is *a particular kind of person* that we can call an 'autistic person', or that there is one distinct *form of autistic life*. This, of course, is as unhelpful and unrealistic as the *mythical norm* that haunts 'the edge of consciousness' (Lorde, 1984: 116), for whom society is mostly designed, but from which most of us diverge in some way or another.

The term *intersectionality* has roots in the Black feminist movement. First coined by critical race theorist Professor Kimberlé Crenshaw in 1989, it describes the ways in which different identity categories (such as race, sex, gender, sexuality and disability) interrelate (or, *intersect*) within an individual: often compounding marginalisation and discrimination. In the context of autism (and wider disability), taking an intersectional view reminds us that 'disability [or: autistic] status is but one part of a person' and that 'the lives of people with disabilities are shaped by various social locations and experiences' (Martino & Schormans, 2018: 12).

Anyone can be autistic, and the category of autism includes people from all kinds of backgrounds and from all walks of life. Sometimes, some of the additional *intersecting* identities that autistic people have, make their being autistic more invisible, meaning that they miss out on formal diagnoses or accommodations and adjustments in employment and education. For some, different aspects of their identities may mean that their life chances are improved, whereas for others these differences may increase the likelihood of them experiencing poor treatment or neglect by society.

In this chapter, we'll touch on some of the different kinds of intersecting, marginalised identities that autistic people may have and, ultimately, think about what that means for cross-neurotype communication. However, when it came to naming these different, intersecting identities, I found it a little difficult. Precisely *because* society privileges certain identities – in particular those most closely aligned with the mythical norm – if you want to talk about those who are most marginalised you end up needing to describe people in terms of the privileges they *don't* have (e.g. people who *aren't* men; people who *aren't* white; people who *aren't* able-bodied). But defining people by *what they're not* diminishes the inherent value of who they actually are and reinforces marginalisation. In the end, I've opted to talk about the ways in which people diverge from different kinds of privileged norms. You may notice they're presented alphabetically. This is because none is more or less important than another.

Diverging from the mythical norm of: *having a gender identity that matches your sex assigned at birth*

Gender – as opposed to *sex* – relates to a socially constructed role that is often described as being learned and performed, and having a cultural component (Butler, 1990). *Sex*, on the other hand, usually relates more to bodies, or to 'biological differences between male and female' (Oakley, 1985: 16), determined (or *assigned*) at birth by observing a newborn's external genitalia[63].

For some people, their gender identity (i.e. an individual's sense of their own gender) doesn't align with the sex assigned to them at birth. We don't have enough information at the moment to know for sure how many people experience this, but the UK 2021 population census (ONS, 2023) can give us a clue. For the first time, a question about respondents' gender identity – *is the gender you identify with the same as your sex registered at birth?* – was introduced. In total, 94% of the UK population over the age of 16 responded to the census, and of these, 262,000 (0.5%) people responded that: no, it did not. Of this group, 48,000 (0.1%) identified as a trans man, 48,000 (0.1%) as a trans woman, and 30,000 (0.06%) as

---

[63] This is fairly abridged summary of what *gender* and *sex* are, and how they relate to one another as constructs. I've tried to keep things simple here, as it's not really within the scope of this book to go into much more detail. However, if you'd like to read more about gender, and more specifically about gender variance – i.e. diverse forms of gender expression – among autistic people, I can highly recommend *Working with Autistic Transgender and Non-binary People*, edited by Marianthi Kourti (2021).

non-binary (i.e. having a gender that doesn't fit neatly into the two binary categories of either male or female).[64]

Trans people in the UK face a lot of stigma and discrimination, as well as considerable health inequities (London Assembly Health Committee, 2022). Most will wait many years before they can begin the process of accessing gender-affirming treatment via the NHS and, in one report, 70% of trans people described experiencing transphobia from their primary care provider, while 14% were outright refused GP care because they were trans (*Ibid*).

Some research has pointed to an increased co-incidence between being both autistic and trans or non-binary (e.g., George & Stokes, 2017; Warrier *et al*, 2020). However, often this research has been 'notably cisgender and neurotypical [...leading to] autistic transgender and non-binary people often not having their identities taken seriously, and not being given the support they need in their own terms' (Kourti, 2021: 17).

From spending a lot of time in autistic spaces, and talking with lots of autistic people, it certainly seems to me that for *many* autistic people, gender can feel a bit... ephemeral. Riffing, here, on time-travelling *Doctor Who's* bemused description of time as a construct: it can sometimes feel like *a big ball of wibbly-wobbly-gendery-wendery stuff*[65]. This vagueness has been picked up elsewhere, for example by Davidson and Tamas (2016) in their analysis of first-hand accounts of autistic people's experiences of their gender, from online surveys, blogs and published autobiographies. They found that:

> '...atypical experiences and expressions of gender are considered relatively common among those on the spectrum. More literal minded than most, many describe meticulous attempts to seek out and solidify gender's troubling manifestations in their social worlds, only to find, of course, that no such thing as gender exists. However, this oddly absent presence continues to haunt autistic emotional lives; its uncanny leavings and doings persist...'
>
> (Davidson & Tamas, 2016: 59)

---

64 Keep in mind that not all trans people may feel safe enough to disclose their trans identity in a census, so these figures may not be fully representative.
65 The 10th Doctor talks about *big ball of wibbly-wobbly, timey-wimey stuff* in the 'Blink' episode (series 3, episode 10: BBC One, 9 June 2007).

More research is needed, but for now, what we can say is that there is a not-insignificant number of autistic people who are trans, non-binary, or have some other form of gender variance. They are perhaps less likely to be believed or taken seriously than non-autistic trans and non-binary people (who already receive inadequate care) and – like all trans people – face additional stigma and health inequities to those experienced by autistic people whose gender aligns with their sex assigned at birth.

Diverging from the mythical norm of: *learning new things easily and living independently*

> 'An extract from Mabel Cooper's records from St Lawrence's Hospital, 1957 read: "Imbecile. A girl of 13 years whose intelligence is not superior to that of the average 7 yr old child. She is educationally very backward, being practically illiterate … She is dull and slow in response, lacks reasoning power and appears to have no general knowledge whatever, being incapable of telling the time." Reflecting on her discovery of these records some years later, Mabel commented: "It did upset me for them to say I wasn't teachable. I think if someone goes around and says something like that, are you going to learn? You are not. And then they turn around and say "Oh you are unteachable".'
>
> (Tilley *et al*, 2021: 347)

The above is an upsetting read, but it is indicative of the way that people with learning disabilities have been perceived and treated throughout history. According to the NHS (NHS England, 2019), people with *learning disabilities* will have a 'significantly reduced ability to understand complex information or learn new skills' and a reduced ability to live independently. Both of these characteristics will have been present before adulthood, and have a 'lasting effect'. *Learning disabilities*, here, are different to what are sometimes referred to as *specific learning disabilities*: things like *dyslexia* (i.e. difficulties in processing written letters) and *dyscalculia* (i.e. difficulties in processing numbers). In the UK, estimates put the figures at just over 2% of the population having a learning disability (NHS England, 2019), with 32.4% of people with learning disabilities also having an autism diagnosis (NHS Digital, 2023).

Hearing from people with disabilities in research has unique barriers, often due to infantilising research ethics procedures that deem people with learning disabilities '"too vulnerable" or "too naïve" ... to make decisions for themselves about participating in research without putting themselves and the researcher(s) at risk' (Santinele Martino and Fudge Schormans, 2018: 1). This is also the case in policy development, where people with learning disabilities are finding themselves framed as beneficiaries of initiatives they had no say in designing, as learning disabled activist Simone Aspis has observed:

'I have noticed that disabled people with learning difficulties are getting left out of projects. When they are part of projects, they are usually given small roles. I think disabled people should be leading the projects. Disabled people should decide how projects are run. All writing should be in an easy read format from the start. Disabled people and speaking up groups should get funding for their own projects.'

(Aspis, 2022)

And yet, hearing what people with learning disabilities have to say about their experiences is of paramount importance. In the UK, while only around 2% of the population is thought to have a learning disability, they represent up to 10% of people in prison (NHS England, 2019). There is also evidence that people with learning disabilities may be more likely to experience homeless (Brown & McCann, 2021). Just like autistic people, people with learning disabilities experience significantly reduced lifespans than people in the general population, with nearly a quarter (22%) of people dying before the age of 50 (Heslop & Glover, 2015). In a Swedish population study already mentioned in this book, Hirvikoski *et al* (2016) found that, while autistic people had reduced lifespans compared to the general population, it was autistic people with co-occurring learning disabilities that died the youngest: at an average age of 39.5 years old.

These are brutal statistics, and ones I hesitated to focus on. However, they make it all the more important to keep autistic people with learning disabilities in mind, and to create opportunities for them to tell us what they need.

Diverging from the mythical norm of: *maleness*

In many ways, it's still a man's world. It's literally *designed* to benefit men – or with men as the default – as Caroline Criado Perez (2019) highlights in her book, *Invisible Women: Exposing data bias in a world designed for men*. From crash-test dummies being built to match the average male dimensions but not accounting for women's bodies, to standard office temperatures being set to men's bodily needs leaving offices feeling an average of 5 degrees too cold for women's requirements, many of the things around us things carry an implicit bias towards men.

This shows up in health data, too. Women – and people assigned female at birth – experience a known 'gender health gap' in Western medicine (DHSC, 2022). Despite having slightly longer average life expectancies, women spend more of life in chronic pain, or with health conditions that go left undiagnosed for longer (Ibid). In one large-scale review, for example, of over 700 diseases, Westergaard *et al* (2019) found that, on average, women were diagnosed around four years later than men. That's four extra years of pain and disease progression. In another study, looking at cardiac diagnoses following a heart attack, researchers found that women are 50% more likely to receive a wrong diagnosis (Wu *et al*, 2018), impinging on their ability to access suitable, sometimes lifesaving, treatment. Female-specific healthcare (e.g. gynaecological and reproductive healthcare) is especially under-researched and under-delivered, exemplified by the fact that *endometriosis* – a painful disease affecting around 10% of women – has a current lag of eight years before an initial diagnosis (that can then trigger a referral to a treatment pathway) is given (APPG on Endometriosis, 2020). Autistic women in particular are at an increased risk of experiencing sub-par reproductive or gynaecological care (Williams *et al*, 2024).

As we saw in Chapter 4, the category of 'autism' was first developed out of the observations of the behaviour of young (white) boys. This seems to have had a lasting impression: from shaping curious explanatory theories for autism such as the *extreme male brain hypothesis* (Baron-Cohen, 2002) to creating 'a lost generation of [women] who were previously excluded from a diagnosis' (Lai and Baron-Cohen, 2015). At present, estimates suggest that boys and men are diagnosed at a rate of 4:1 compared to girls and women (Lord *et al*, 2020). This historically accumulative diagnostic gap is a worry: with many women in mid and later life left in limbo while they either sit it out in impossibly long waiting lists for assessments (Westminster Commission on Autism, 2021) or, when they do finally receive a diagnosis, are left without any post-diagnostic support (Crane *et al*, 2018).

The diagnostic disparities faced by autistic girls and women are definitely a systemic problem, but they may be compounded by the increased tendency for autistic girls and women to build public identities that *camouflage* or *mask* their autistic traits (McQuaid *et al*, 2022), meaning that diagnosticians may miss them if they're not trained to look past this. 'Ella' – a participant in an Australian study investigating late-diagnosed autistic women's wellbeing (Seers & Hogg, 2022) – describes this imperative to self-protect:

> *'I knew that I was different, I knew that I wasn't like other people, and I sort of tried to blend in as much as was humanely possible. Society's not kind. If I had of [sic] stood out, then maybe I would have been bullied.'*
>
> (Ella, in Seers & Hogg, 2022: 6)

It is not just adult autistic women who have been – and often still are – invisible, but autistic girls too. Girls are typically diagnosed later than boys (Lai *et al*, 2022) and often only once a secondary mental health condition brings them to services (Wilkinson, 2008). Even when they *do* have a diagnosis, autistic girls are often less likely to receive appropriate support in mainstream schools, in part *due* to their coping skills, including masking (Halsall *et al*, 2021).

While there does seem to be improving understanding and public awareness of how being autistic and female (or assigned female at birth) looks, there is still a long way to go.

Diverging from the mythical norm of: *using spoken words fluently*

As I explained in the introduction, this book has focused its attention on communication that takes place between two speakers. However, some estimates say that around 25-30% of autistic people don't use spoken words to communicate all (or almost all) of the time (Rose et al, 2016)[66].

Historically – just like those with learning disabilities – those unable to use spoken words to communicate and advocate for themselves have been infantilised, confined to institutions, and assumed to have intellectual and cognitive 'impairments' that severely reduce the possibility for a meaningful quality of life or capacity for thought[67]. In other words: they have been dehumanised.

Thankfully, we are in a *slightly* better place today. Reflecting this, in recent years there has been a slow but steady increase in the number of published texts written by non-speaking autistic people who have learned to use (sometimes incredibly effortful) alternative and augmentative means to communicate, or who developed spoken communication at a later age (see Appendix for a list of books, blogs and other resources). Many of these are autobiographical, reflexive accounts that illuminate their experiences of being non-speaking.

One such text, originally written in Japanese, is *The Reason I Jump* by (a then) 13-year-old, non-speaking Naoki Higashida. Having spent much of his childhood deeply frustrated by not being able to communicate with those around him, Higashida eventually learned to communicate by painstakingly pointing out words, letter by letter, on a letter grid: taking between 60 seconds and 20 minutes to complete a sentence. One day, British author and father to a non-speaking son, David Mitchell, stumbled across Higashida's work on the internet and began corresponding with him about translating the writing into English. While the translation enjoyed a largely positive reception:

> '...an accusation was levelled that nobody with "genuine" severe [sic] autism could possibly have authored such articulate prose: never

---

66 Keep in mind with any such percentages, we aren't *really* sure how many people are autistic in the first place.
67 E.g. see: *Letter to Adelheid Bloch* in Joanne Limburg's (2021) *Letters To My Weird Sisters: On Autism and Feminism*.

mind the YouTube clips showing Naoki authoring this same articulate prose... Therefore, Naoki must have been misdiagnosed and doesn't have autism at all; or he's an impostor at the Asperger's syndrome end of the spectrum, akin to the character Sheldon Cooper in The Big Bang Theory; or his books are written by someone else, possibly his mother. Or me.'

(Mitchell, 2017: online)

This kind of scepticism surrounding people who type to communicate and the legitimacy of their authorship is unfortunately still commonplace (Williams, 2020). It sometimes shows up in high-stakes settings, such as in healthcare environments, where being non-speaking can be mistaken for not having capacity (Williams *et al*, 2022), leading to a loss of autonomy over medical procedures, treatment and consent.

It's not completely clear why some people are non-speaking. In some cases, speech production is thought to be hampered by *verbal apraxia* (sometimes accompanied by general *apraxia*) – a neurological condition in which the language system and the motor system involved in speech articulation struggle to connect up. Non-speaking people know exactly what they'd like to say but can't make it happen.

In a co-produced report about communicating effectively with autistic people in healthcare settings (Williams *et al*, 2022), one of the collaborators – a semi-speaking person called Helen – shares her experience of exactly that kind of frustration:

'Myself and others that experience verbal apraxia describe it as – your brain is saying, do this, and your body is doing something you didn't even predict or want to do. For example, an autistic with significant apraxia may want to say "I really don't want to be here now" but instead will come out with "give me Pringles!!" or they might end up having total block of speech production and instead scream and jump onto a table.'

(Helen, 2022: 10)

Despite the advancement in alternative and augmentative communication (AAC) technologies – which, as Sararvese (2021) points out, are not affordable by all who need them – our world still privileges those who are both hearing and speaking (and not those who are deaf or non-speaking). Because spoken communication mediates so much of our social interactions, autistic people who are also non-speaking may find themselves at an even higher risk of experiencing social isolation and loneliness.

Diverging from the mythical norm of: *whiteness*

> 'When I – as a black person, as a woman, as an autistic adult, as the mother of black autistic children, as an advocate – think about the world of autism research and practice, the words of Doughboy come to mind. In a poignant ending scene from the late African American director John Singleton's iconic debut film, Boyz n the Hood, Doughboy sadly remarks, "Either they don't know, don't show... or don't care about what's going on in the hood." Similarly, when it comes to autism, either they – or should I say you all – do not know, do not show, or do not care about black, indigenous, people of color (BIPoC) very much.'
>
> (Giwa Onaiwu, 2020: 270)

We have touched on this elsewhere in the book, but it bears repeating: *autism research has a race problem* (Jones *et al*, 2020). Studies are designed and delivered by autism researchers who are predominantly white (Jones *et al*, 2020; Giwa Onaiwu, 2020), and populated by research participants who are, in turn, also predominantly white. In a large-scale systematic review of the autism intervention literature published between 1990 and 2017 (Steinbrenner *et al*, 2022), the authors found that only 25% of studies reported the race and ethnicity of their participants. Of those that were reported, Black, Hispanic/Latino, and Asian participants made up only 7.7%, 9.4%, and 6.4%, respectively, across all included participants. Worryingly, these low figures appear to represent a drop from still low, but slightly higher numbers reported by West *et al* in 2016: suggesting that the inclusion of racially minoritised participants is decreasing, rather than improving (Steinbrenner *et al*, 2022). This picture is complicated further by the fact that Black, Brown and racially minoritised people face significant biases in accessing autism (Begeer *et al*, 2009; Cascio *et al*, 2020).

As such, a lot remains unknown; for example, the different ways that autism may present among people who are racially minoritised, or how these identities may intersect. For example, *code-switching* is a phenomenon whereby Black people moderate their appearance as well as the way they speak when moving into white spaces – e.g. moving from Black British English, Multicultural London English or African American English to Standard British or Standard American English – in order to preserve their safety (Grehoua, 2020; Wyatt & Seymour, 1988; Young 2009). Autistic people, too, undertake *masking* or *camouflaging* behaviours (Hull *et al*, 2017; Pearson & Rose, 2023) but we don't really know how *code-switching* and *masking* may influence one another, and at what cost to the autistic person. Where things *are* known – such as the racial and ethnic disparities in access to autism-related support and health care (Liu *et al*, 2023) – they are 'rarely, if ever, applied in a manner that could result in meaningful change' (Giwa Onaiwu, 2020: 270).

Whether it's comfortable to admit or not, we live in a racialised society. And as many have pointed out, this white privilege problem is not confined to autism research. In media depictions as well as public understanding, 'the typical "face" of autism tends to be that of a little white boy' (Giwa Onaiwu, 2020: 270). Those who are both autistic and racially minoritised, face a 'double minority status' (Cascio *et al*, 2020) that shows up in all walks of life:

> 'With racism, I had to fight to get my diagnosis, and even now, there are people – mostly White people – who refuse to accept it. Medical racism is something that I am always having to confront, even as an immigrant in the United Kingdom. Every aspect of trying to live, even just a bare minimum good life, is still a fight...'
> (Ms Ellwood, in Jones *et al*, 2020: 274)

In addition to facing increased health inequities, Black autistic people are at a significantly increased risk of harm, often perpetrated by those in positions of authority who should be there to help. Numerous cases have been reported in the news of Black autistic boys and men being incarcerated or brutalised by police who have misinterpreted their autistic ways of being as indicators of threatening behaviour (Hutson *et al*, 2022). In the US and some other parts of the world, these encounters carry a material risk of death (Ibid). In the UK this is less likely, but encounters with law enforcement remain dangerous. For example, in 2022, a 17-year-old Black and non-speaking autistic boy was detained in a facility at Gatwick airport and told he would be deported to Nigeria:

> 'The boy, who is not Nigerian and has no connection to the country, had been reported missing by his family and was later arrested by the British Transport Police for alleged fare evasion. Because he had no identification and was unable to speak, he was detained at an immigration centre.
>
> '"They locked him up like a prisoner and mishandled him," his sister wrote on Twitter. "When they saw my brother, they didn't see a boy in pain, they saw his race".'
>
> (Phillip, 2022: online)

Finally, in the most recent reporting of government data, Black people were identified as being nearly five times as likely as white people to be detained under the Mental Health Act (342 detentions for every 100,000 people, compared with 72 for every 100,000 people: Gov.UK, 2023), resulting in prolonged periods of incarceration in mental health facilities and a removal of personal autonomy. While we don't know how many of these individuals were autistic – because it has not been reported, and because of systemic underdiagnosis of Black and Brown autistic people – we can be sure that some of them were.

Diverging from the mythical norm: *of youth*

> 'Who will look after me if I need care? How will I survive a long stay in a hospital? Will a care home pressure me to join in social activities because that is what neurotypical people want? How will I be judged by my peer residents, if I don't make small-talk or gossip? If sensory overload or anxiety leads to a meltdown, will I be shunted straight to the dementia ward?'
>
> (Cos Michael, autistic advocate, 2016: 515)

The first generation of autistic people diagnosed in childhood (such as Donald Triplett) are now reaching older adulthood, but our knowledge of what ageing as an autistic person looks like is virtually non-existent. And yet, the UK has an ageing population (Walker, 2018), replete with autistic people moving towards an age at which they may require additional supports.

With better public understanding of autism, many adults are now seeking diagnoses in mid- and later life, but older autistic people remain disproportionately under-diagnosed (Autistica, 2019). Many may have spent a lifetime masking, or they may not know that they *are* autistic. As such, at present, adult social care services in the UK are 'currently likely to know only a small number' (Social Care, Local Government and Care Partnership Directorate, 2014: 25) of all local autistic people, as the majority will not have previously engaged with services. According to the Social Care Institute for Excellence (2017), just 35,000-58,000 autistic people (across the whole life course) are known to social care services, mostly by virtue of their co-occurring learning disabilities. For the many autistic individuals without co-occurring learning disabilities or acute mental health needs, access routes to social care services are 'blocked' (2017: 8), often by service provider misapprehension about needs.

While many older autistic people will have similar needs to non-autistic older people, there are potentially areas where these needs may diverge. For example, older autistic people who have benefitted from the support of parent- or sibling-carers may become disproportionately dependent on social care in later life (Michael, 2016; Wake *et al*, 2021) when these carers are no longer able to support them. Others who have previously managed without support may now find themselves in need as they face the challenge of a transition into a new phase of life (Social Care Institute for Excellence, 2017). Additional autism-specific ageing difficulties may include potential sensory distress in residential care facilities with aversive sensory environments or divergent communication and distress responses that may be mistaken for dementia (Crompton *et al*, 2020).

Despite all this, there remains a dearth of autism research focused on older autistic people (Mason *et al*, 2022). Of the limited research that has been undertaken so far, the majority addresses difficulties in accessing diagnoses in later life or highlights the lack of knowledge about autism and ageing (Happé & Charlton, 2012). A very limited number of empirical studies have been published, and those that have tend to focus on things like brain structure and function and genetics rather than quality of life or care needs (Mason *et al*, 2022). As we saw in Wong *et al*'s (2017) work, older people can often come to feel alienated through a gradual but growing distance from their previous identities and social connections. For older autistic people, the risk of alienation is surely higher, and the uncertainty around what to expect – both in terms of the ageing process itself and the support that may or may not be provided – can be a frightening prospect.

Further and multiply intersecting identities

The intersections named above are just a few of the possible ways in which an autistic individual can additionally diverge from the mythical norm. Autistic people can be both able-bodied and disabled. They may have mental health concerns, chronic pain, or physical health problems. In fact, there is a relatively new and growing body of evidence that suggests that neurodivergence often co-occurs with connective tissue disorders (see Csecs *et al*, 2022). They may come from socio-economic backgrounds that afford them access to private autism diagnostic assessments, or they may not – in which case, if they live in the UK, they will have to wait in an ever-lengthening NHS queue (Westminster Commission on Autism, 2021) before they're seen. In the US, one study (Durkin *et al*, 2017) computed rates of diagnosed autistic people among different demographic groups and found that, as well as significant ethnic and racial disparities, economically disadvantaged groups were routinely under-diagnosed. Autistic people may come from faith backgrounds and communities that have a bearing on how they feel about being autistic, and how comfortable they feel being known as being autistic. As we've seen, not all autistic people have fixed abodes. Autistic people have very diverse educational backgrounds. Some autistic people may be fat[68] and some may be thin. The list goes on…

Finally, different marginalised identities can – and do – stack up and uniquely influence one another: an idea at the core of intersectional thinking. Autistic people do not, as a general rule, tend to have it easy in our society. We know this. But some will have it harder than others. Any additional, marginalised, intersecting identities that an autistic person has will have the potential to make their life harder. This is especially vital to keep in mind when it comes to listening to autistic people. If we are to begin the process of *world-building* (Stauffer, 2015), we need to prioritise

---

[68] *Fattism* – the discrimination and stigmatisation of people on the grounds of having larger bodies – is often described as the 'last acceptable prejudice' (Solanke, 2022: 125).

the voices of those with multiple marginalisations who have, historically, been heard the least.

Intersectional identities and cross-neurotype communication

Anything that forms part of our unique, individual social positioning and context will ultimately influence what's in our cognitive environment. When two individuals come together, the more 'different' we are from one another – including the more diverging, intersectional aspects of our identities – the less our cognitive environments overlap. Our mutual cognitive environment is therefore smaller, with less being mutually manifest.

This isn't a deal breaker for achieving mutual understanding, but more (cognitive) effort will likely be required when undertaking the search for relevance. As we follow the well-worn track of *weighing up cognitive efforts spent versus positive cognitive effects gained*, we may need to be willing to spend a little more to get what we want.

This, somehow, reminds me of something Audre Lorde had to say about difference, and how approaching it face-on can take us to new places:

> 'Difference must not merely be tolerated, but seen as a fund of necessary polarities between which our creativity can spark like a dialectic. Only then does the necessity for interdependency become unthreatening. Only within that interdependency of different strengths, acknowledged and equal, can the power to seek new ways of being in the world generate, as well as the courage and sustenance to act where there are no charters.'
>
> (Lorde, 1984: 111)

We are interdependent beings[69], coerced by a profit economy into thinking that our differences are a threat. Lorde (1984: 115), again:

> 'As members of such an economy we have all been programmed to respond to the human differences between us with fear and loathing and to handle that difference in one of three ways: ignore it, and if

---

69 *My sovereignty depends.*

that is not possible, copy it if we think it is dominant, or destroy it if we think it is subordinate.'

And yet, we each have the potential to change our reactions to those who are different to ourselves: to others. We can choose, to engage, to listen, to make the extra efforts and co-create new norms, new ways of being in the world.

In the final chapter, we'll think about what this might look like in more practical terms.

Chapter 11: Towards a connected, inclusive society

And here we are, the final chapter. We've come a long way since the start of this book. We started out by thinking about the ways in which cognising beings interact with the world(s) around them, thinking, in particular, about the embodied and enactive basis of cognition. We then looked at how cognisors communicate relevant information to one another, and compared the code model vs. the ostensive-inferential model of communication. We thought about *meaning*, and dug through the nuts and bolts of relevance theory: a cognitive account of utterance interpretation that hinges on the fact that we need to sift out the information that is relevant to us in a data-saturated world. We've looked at autism theories from the medical model as well as the social model of disability and covered a short history of research into autistic language use. We homed in on the double empathy problem and looked at parallel theories from other disciplines before exploring how relevance theory might help explain what's going on, in cognitive linguistic terms. Finally, we've considered the impact on autistic people of not being heard or understood and how that might have a compounding effect on those from additionally minoritised backgrounds.

The overarching message may have perhaps seemed to be that autistic and non-autistic people exist in different worlds, and that communication between the two will always be hindered by a double empathy problem. I hope that's not the message I've conveyed. While, it's true, autistic and non-autistic people do often experience (and enact) their worlds in different ways and, as such, have potentially markedly divergent cognitive environments, it's very possible to make communication work, with a little extra effort.

In Chapter 6, for example, we looked at the findings from some research I'd undertaken as part of my doctorate degree (Williams *et al*, 2021). Autistic and non-autistic people had been invited to come and talk, in mixed pairs about loneliness – both their own experience of it and their impressions about loneliness in the local city. As already discussed, conversations between pairings of autistic participants – even when they were strangers to one another – were characterised by flow, rapport and intersubjective attunement. However, mutual understanding was also unexpectedly high across all types of conversation pairings: including those involving cross-neurotype, stranger matchings. Even in some of these latter pairings, we saw high levels of rapport and interpersonal attunement.

This, I'm sure, will not be the only piece of research that points to autistic and non-autistic people finding ways to communicate rewardingly. We also see it all around us. We do live in a neurodiverse world and across all dimensions of life there are examples of cross-neurotype mutual flourishing: in friendships, in workplaces, in homes and in hearts. We may need to approach things a little differently, but it absolutely can (and does) work.

Connecting in the borderlands (or the 'Third Space')

In a co-produced narrative account documenting the journey of an autistic woman through speech and language therapy (Walsh *et al*, 2018), the authors – the autistic client, her speech and language therapist and a clinical supervisor – describe using 'the figurative notion of [the] *borderland*' to situate a nontraditional, collaborative way of working together. The autistic client (Patricia) was a late-diagnosed autistic woman who had sought out the assistance of a speech-language pathologist to help her with 'stressful and anxiety-provoking communication challenges' (2018: 108). The practitioner (Irene) wanted to approach the difficulties Patricia was experiencing in making herself understood in a manner that both moved away from a traditional speech-language pathology thinking about 'deficits', and that was truly collaborative. In working together in an intentionally more equal and flexible way, purposefully undoing the traditional power balance of 'expert clinician treating an impaired patient' (2018: 108), they co-created a borderland space:

> 'The borderland was characterized by the orientations or stances of the participants in these settings, in this case, [Patricia] who was seeking help in an open-minded way, and [Irene] who was exploring a different way of working alongside [autistic people]. This borderland then is created at the edges of these worlds and

constructed by the people who occupied this space, bringing to it their values and beliefs from their respective cultures, identities, and concerns. Thus, the cultural–clinical borderland takes on the characteristics of a more flexible space, where the boundaries are less rigid and where the shared goal is the "creation of common ground".
(Walsh et al, 2018: 111)

The *borderland* is one of several rich metaphors for a particular kind of (inter-)psychological state in which interactions across some kind of *difference* take place. We often find such metaphors in texts that talk about intercultural encounters. For example, in the *English as a Lingua Franca* literature, we see Young and Sachdev's (2011) notion of a *third culture*. English as a Lingua Franca, you might remember, is English used between speakers for whom English is not their first language. As such, English as a Lingua Franca encounters often involve speakers from different language backgrounds and different cultural backgrounds. A core characteristic of English as a Lingua Franca communication is its typically consensual nature, with new norms emerging and being perpetuated throughout the interaction. Within these encounters, multiple identities and social group memberships are at play simultaneously – including professional roles and hierarchies, cultural and national stereotypes (which can be positive, negative and neutral), gender and race. Yet in addition to all of these, there is also a mutual awareness of a *shared* identity – the identity of being non-native speakers and of communicating in an intercultural, borderland space.

Being a successful *intercultural speaker* involves being able to navigate these different identities, and to do that, speakers must find a way of appropriately mediating between a 'world of origin and [a] world of encountered difference' (Young & Sachdev, 2011: 83):

'*Such mediation involves the affective and cognitive capacity to establish and maintain relationships with individuals from a different culture [...] At the heart of this conceptualisation lies the belief that intercultural competence involves successfully mediating between cultures, the first culture, or "C1", that an individual was enculturated into, and a second, other culture, or "C2", so that an individual aims to occupy a relativising [third culture, or] "C3g".*'

This idea of a *third culture* sounds, to me, quite like post-colonial scholar Homi K Bhabha's (1987) concept of the *Third Space,* a concept he developed while thinking about historical and geographical sites of cultural translation (e.g. encounters between Christian Evangelical missionaries and native Hindus in Northern India in the 19th century). According to Bhabha, encounters between individuals from two different social groups 'with different traditions and potentials of power' constitute 'a special kind of negotiation or translation' (Ikas & Wagner, 2009). These unique kinds of cultural interfacing are thought to be 'enunciated' in a *third space or boundary: 'a place from which something begins its presencing'* (Bhabha, 1994: 5).

In each of these descriptions of borderland and third spaces, then, is the potentiality of newness. By opening ourselves to difference, we create the opportunity to find new common ground hitherto unimagined. And yet the third space or borderland cannot be entered into if it isn't conceived of as such.

All too often, in encounters across difference, it is the shoulders of the minority subject onto which the labour of adjustment and reconciliation falls. For those individuals whose ways of being are at odds with that of the majority, there is a greater imperative to bridge the gap, so as to not be left misunderstood, to not be overlooked, but to be heard. In her book titled *Borderlands: La Frontera,* Anzaldúa (1987) – a lesbian, bilingual Chicana growing up at the Texas/ Mexico border – describes her experience not in terms of being 'other', but as being 'a border woman', needing to shift gears at any moment:

> *'Not only [is] the brain split into two functions but so [is] reality. Thus people who inhabit both realities are forced to live at the interface between the two, forced to become adept at switching modes.'*
> (Anzaldúa, 1987: 59)

For many, the imperative to code-switch or mask at a moment's notice carries a greater weight, as Lorde reminds us:

> *'Traditionally [...] it is the members of oppressed, objectified groups who are expected to stretch out and bridge the gap between the*

*actualities of our lives and the consciousness of our oppressor.
In order to survive, those of us for whom oppression is as american
[sic] as apple pie have to become watchers, to become familiar
with the language and manners of the oppressor, even sometimes
adopting them...'*

(Lorde, 1984: 114)

We see a similar burden of change falling on autistic people too, in the form of ABA (Applied Behavioural Analysis) interventions for autistic children and enforced social skills training. For some, this may be desired and beneficial, but for most it simply tries to squash autistic round pegs into non-autistic square holes.

In cross-neurotype communication, it is almost always the autistic person who is expected to adapt to the norms of society so that they may participate. It is they who must make, or be willing to make, the extra cognitive efforts in order to blend in, and have their needs met. But from what we know of the double empathy problem, there is often a *two-way* difficulty of understanding between autistic and non-autistic people. And, from relevance theory, we know that either speaker can make the wrong assumptions about what is mutually manifest. With this knowledge, an opportunity really opens up for non-autistic parties to take the lead in trying to accommodate, to establish a third space, or to make the extra efforts in their search for relevance, to understand better what autistic people say...

Connecting practically

If the above is a little ephemeral, let's think about it in more practical terms. If you're not autistic and you're reading this, what can you do to be a more helpful ally and to improve the chances of communication with autistic people going well?

The most valuable thing you can do, really, is to try to *tune in* to the autistic person before you, to try to understand where they're coming from. It's something like how you might approach listening to the radio spoken in another language – one you're familiar with but pretty rusty on – trying to tune your ear to identify the essential intended message without getting caught up worrying about the grammar or every word.

It's something like the attitude of openness, receptivity and respect for individual differences that sits at the heart of successful intercultural communication, that being willing to *go on with* another person (and that willingness to make a little extra effort to identify what they want you to understand). It's something like how users of English as a Lingua Franca reach out and build new norms with every new English as a Lingua Franca interaction they have, how in-jokes are formed, and linguistic infelicities – or things that don't quite make sense – are let to pass.

Finally, try to find something that you both have in common and that you can enthuse over, and allow that to pull you into sync with one another. For our study, talking about loneliness seemed to function that way, so it may be that entering into frank, open conversations is the way to go, but it might also be that finding something you can both focus on (oh! A bird!) might do it. The point, perhaps, is to explore, to be adventuresome, to enter into communication with the ambition of building a new (third) communicative world. Run along the edges of meaning, like Aaron and his mother (as we saw in Chapter 5) and allow yourself to fall into a sensory mode of experiencing language, to play...

More than words

If you'd like something a little more prescriptive and actionable, I and some colleagues may also be able to help. Over the course of 2022, I worked in collaboration with 16 others to co-produce some guidelines for communicating well with autistic people in healthcare settings. Our group was made up of autistic healthcare service users – some of whom are autistic advocates or activists, autistic healthcare professionals and healthcare educators, and non-autistic healthcare professionals and strategic leads. Two of our group were semi-speaking. We met over Zoom, several times over several months and came up with a set of ten recommendations, with the hope that these could be used as the basis for *reasonable* and *anticipatory adjustments* in healthcare settings. *Reasonable adjustments* are adaptations to services that can be made to ensure individuals with protected characteristics aren't disadvantaged in accessing them. Adjustments must be reasonable and relevant to each individual and this is built into UK law in the Equality Act and the Autism Act. *Anticipatory adjustments* are adaptations service providers can put into place in advance of patients requesting them: for example, providing closed captions for recorded audio, or providing the opportunity to book appointments online rather than over the phone.

While our recommendations are focused on healthcare settings, many of them are transferrable to other contexts: like employment, education, even for social encounters. You might also find them helpful to take along to share with your healthcare provider if you're autistic, or if your loved one is. The report is free to access and available online (see p.191), but our recommendations are summarised below:

Recommendation 1: Always consider that a patient [or someone you're talking to] may be autistic.

Anyone can be autistic and this may not necessarily be obvious when you first meet your patient [or the person before you]. Where you have a sense it might be a possibility, err on the side of caution and look to make reasonable adjustments: in particular to communication and the sensory environment.

Recommendation 2: Adapt the sensory environment to support autistic people to engage and communicate comfortably with services [or to feel at ease wherever you're hoping to engage with them].

Healthcare premises [and lots of public spaces] can often be overwhelming sensory environments for autistic people. Wherever possible, make reasonable adjustments to the sensory environment such as turning off bright lights, offering a quiet space to wait, or permitting headphones and sunglasses on wards [or in classrooms, etc.]. Take sensory sensitivities into consideration when interacting with your autistic patients [or autistic people in general] and try to avoid adding to overwhelm by giving them lots of spoken information delivered quickly. Allow autistic patients [or people, generally] time to ground themselves and process what's being communicated: even where distress is not evident to you.

Recommendation 3: When taking a history from autistic patients [or, when you're asking autistic people about how they feel in themselves] consider whether atypical interoception (e.g. a reduced awareness of bodily sensations) may be affecting how (and what) symptoms [or experiences] are reported.

This is a common co-occurring sensory difference many autistic people experience [and particularly in healthcare settings, it may mean they're not describing things, such as pain, in ways you might expect].

Recommendation 4: Wherever possible, create a reliable, predictable environment and support 'single-focused' attention.

[In healthcare settings:] keep autistic patients updated with wait times and their changing place in a queue. Remember that autistic people often have a single-focused attention style and need activities to unfold one-by-one rather than simultaneously (e.g. talk to your patients before examining them, rather than at the same time). [Focus on one topic at a time and reduce other competing forms of attention-grabbing stimuli.]

Recommendation 5: Be aware that some autistic people will lose their ability to speak.

Look out for signs that your autistic patient [or friend, or loved one, or student, or colleague...] is losing their ability to speak in the moment. Provide a calm and quiet environment for them to re-regulate, be mindful of adding to overwhelm, and offer and support alternative means of communication (such as written modes). Don't assume that your autistic patient [or friend, or colleague...] has understood what you've said just because they are using words if they seem overwhelmed. Use checking questions and active listening techniques.

Recommendation 6: Support non-speakers to use AAC and always assume capacity.

Factor in extra time to allow semi-speaking and non-speaking autistic people to use Alternative and Augmentative Communication (AAC) methods. Be mindful that barriers to using speech can be related to verbal apraxia and [are not a sign of] lack of capacity.

Recommendation 7: Think about communication challenges as a two-way mismatch when interacting with autistic patients and make efforts to 'meet them in the middle'.

Autistic people will have spent much of their lives not being understood, so take the time to put them at ease and show that you are listening and interested. One way to bridge the double empathy problem is to imagine that the autistic patient [or person] before you may have a vastly different experience of thinking, speaking, listening, seeing, and knowing their feelings: and begin from here.

Recommendation 8: Pay attention to what autistic people say about their pain and symptoms, and resist making clinical judgements based solely on behavioural signifiers [or, resist making assumptions about how your autistic friend, student, partner, etc., may be feeling based solely on how they appear to be behaving].

Autistic people often have atypical body language and facial expressions which can lead to them not being believed when they report symptoms [or when they describe how they feel about things]. Considering the significant health inequities that autistic people face [and the burden of ethical loneliness], always err on the side of caution.

Recommendation 9: Consider a trauma-informed care approach when working with all autistic patients [or therapeutic clients, or students, etc].

Autistic people are much more likely than the general population to experience traumatic experiences that can result in post-traumatic stress disorder which can become a further barrier to accessing services [or attending school, showing up to the Mosque or Church, etc.]. Taking a trauma-informed care approach as standard practice [or just a trauma-informed approach], built on the principles of safety, choice, collaboration, trustworthiness and empowerment, can support autistic patients [or, people] to access services.

> **Recommendation 10: Offer a variety of methods for making appointments and accessing services.**
>
> Having to use the telephone to book an appointment can be a significant barrier for many autistic people. To enable equitable access to services for autistic patients (diagnosed, undiagnosed and undisclosed), alternative methods of booking appointments – by text, email or an accessible online booking system – should be offered from the outset to all patients.
>
> Adapted from: Gemma Williams, Helen Cave, Jamie + Lion, Jon Adams, Karen Forrest, Mary Doherty, Nick Chown, Peter Bull, Rachel Fricker, Ria Foster, Rosie Murray, Sebastian C. K. Shaw, Tish Marrable, Tré Ventour-Griffiths (2022: 3-4)

Above all, I would say that an attitude of openness and friendly curiosity really will go a long way. As will keeping in mind our human tendency to form quick, thin-slice, negative judgments about those who are different to ourselves, and our built-in mechanism to stop looking for relevant interpretations as soon as we think we've found the most obvious (i.e. first) one. Give cross-neurotype interactions a little space, a little time, and you might be pleasantly surprised. The autistic person you're talking to certainly will be.

A final word: connecting productively

> *'The borderline work of culture demands an encounter with 'newness' that is not part of the continuum of past and present. It creates a sense of the new as an insurgent act of cultural translation.'*
>
> (Bhabha, 1994: 7)

This book has, I hope, provided a kind of technical explanation for why communication may sometimes slip up between speakers of different neurotypes. We've looked at how relevance theory might help us make sense of the double empathy problem and how, in turn, it can help us know how to approach cross-neurotype interactions differently.

Now, here is my *non-technical* opinion:

When we engage in cross-neurotype communication, we are talking between worlds. If we do this right (and with a little luck) a third world opens up: one populated by objects of both the known and the *other* world. Sometimes these remain as a delicious new mix of disparate representations, but sometimes they are blended together and made totally anew. This is more than translation. It is transmutation[70].

It is like the honeybee, pressing her body deep into the flower to seek out nectar. The flower is changed (it will either yield or receive pollen, depending on its sex, thus taking part in plant reproduction), the bee is changed (she is now replete with nourishing plant fluids) but, ultimately, a new, third thing will spring from this glorious cross-species interaction: golden, health-giving, honey.

---

70 Or magic.

Appendix 1: List of resources from non-speaking and semi-speaking autistic advocates

This book has focused on one particular way of thinking about the breakdowns in understanding that can sometimes occur during spoken interactions between autistic and non-autistic people. However, there are a huge number of autistic people who do not have access to reliable or fluent speech, and who do not use spoken language to communicate for the majority of the time. Some never use spoken words. It feels important to include their voices and perspectives here, as they face additional barriers to being heard and understood on a daily basis.

Below you will find the beginnings of a list of resources either made by or featuring non-speaking and semi-speaking autistic people, as they are the experts on their own experiences. There are no doubt many great resources missed here, and for that I can only apologise. This list is by no means exhaustive, but I hope it can open some new doors to fresh perspectives and new insights on communicating without spoken words…

Interviews with non-speaking or semi-speaking autistic people:
'Niko Boskovic – Letterboarding Leader':
www.spectrumlife.org/blog/niko-boskovic-letterboarding-leader

Websites of groups and organisations:
Ask Me I'm an AAC User (Facebook Group):
www.facebook.com/groups/456220758119314

Communication 4 ALL:
https://communication4all.org/

CommunicationFIRST:
https://communicationfirst.org/

Websites and blogs belonging to individuals:

Jordan Zimmerman:
www.jordynzimmerman.com/

Sabrina Guerra, Non-Speaking Advocate for Change:
www.facebook.com/SabrinaGuerraNonspeakingAdvocate/about

Alyssa Hillary Zisk:
https://yesthattoo.blogspot.com/

@endeverstar:
https://anotherqueerautistic.wordpress.com/

Oliver – The Tudors Make Me Tic:
https://thetudorsmakemetic.com/

Hari Srinivasan:
https://uniquelyhari.blogspot.com/

Amy Sequenzia:
https://ollibean.com/author/amy-sequenzia/

Danny Whitty:
https://dannywithwords.com/

Ido Kellar:
http://idoinautismland.com/

Videos and films:

'Listen':
www.youtube.com/watch?v = H7dca7U7GI8

'This Is Not About Me':
https://thisisnotaboutme.film/watch/

'See Us, Hear Us Campaign':
https://communicationfirst.org/see-us-hear-us/

'Loop' (Pixar Shorts)

Selected books:

The Reason I Jump, by Higashida Naoki

Typed Words, Loud Voices, edited by Amy Sequenzia and Elizabeth J Grace

Life in Letters: A Book About Autism, by Lia Assimakopoulos

AUTISTIC & AWESOME: A Journal from the Inside, by Alfonso Julián Camacho

In Two Worlds, by Ido Kellar

Ido in Autismland: Climbing Out of Autism's Silent Prison, by Ido Kellar

The Mind Tree: A Miraculous Child Breaks the Silence of Autism, by Tito Rajarshi Mukhopadhyay

Communication Alternatives in Autism: Perspectives on Typing and Spelling Approaches for the Nonspeaking, edited by Edlyn Vallejo Peña

The Autistic Mind Finally Speaks: Letterboard Thoughts, by Gregory Tino

For more resources by non-speaking autistic people, see NeuroClastic's fantastic and extensive directory: (https://neuroclastic.com/directory-of-nonspeaker-pages-blogs-media/).

Appendix 2

'Notational conventions employed in the transcribed excerpts [replicated in Chapter 5] include the following:

.	Period indicates a falling, or final, intonation contour, not necessarily the end of a sentence.
?	Question mark indicates rising intonation, not necessarily a question.
,	Comma indicates "continuing" intonation, not necessarily a clause boundary.
↑↓	Upward and downward pointing arrows indicate marked rising and falling shifts in intonation.
→	Right facing arrow indicates lines in the transcript where the phenomenon of interest occurs.
:::	Colons indicate stretching of the preceding sound, proportional to the number of colons.
-	A hyphen after a word or a part of a word indicates a cut-off or self interruption.
<u>wo</u>rd	Underlining indicates some form of stress or emphasis on the underlined item.
WOrd	Upper case indicates loudness.
=	Equal sign indicate no break or delay between the words thereby connected.
(( ))	Double parentheses enclose descriptions of conduct.
(word)	When all or part of an utterance is in parentheses, this indicates uncertainty on the transcriber's part.
( )	Empty parentheses indicate that something is being said, but no hearing can be achieved.

(1.2)   Numbers in parentheses indicate silence in tenths of a second.

(.)   A dot in parentheses indicated a "micropause," hearable but not readily measurable; ordinarily less than 2/10 of a second.

[Separate left square brackets, one above the other on two successive lines with utterances by different speakers, indicates a point of overlap onset.'

(From: Sterponi & Fasulo, 2018: 139)

References

Introduction
Abram, D. (1996) *The Spell of the Sensuous: Language and Perception in a More than Human World*. New York: Pantheon

Chapter 1
Clark, A. (1997) *Being There: Putting Brain, Body, and World Together Again*. Massachusetts: MIT Press.

Clark, A. (2013) Whatever next? Predictive brains, situated agents, and the future of cognitive science. *Behavioral and Brain Sciences*, **36** (3): 181-204

Descartes, R. (1998) *Meditations and Other Metaphysical Writings* (Clarke, D. trans.) London: Penguin

Di Paolo, E.A., Cuffari, E.C. and De Jaegher, H. (2018) *Linguistic Bodies: The Continuity between Life and Language*. Massachusetts: MIT Press

Maturana, H.R. and Varela, F.J. (1991) *Autopoiesis and cognition: The realization of the living* (Vol. 42). Springer Science & Business Media

Seth, A.K. and Tsakiris, M. (2018) Being a beast machine: The somatic basis of selfhood. *Trends in Cognitive Sciences*, **22** (11): 969-981

Varela, F. Thompson, E., and Rosch, E. (1991) *The Embodied Mind: Cognitive Science and Human Experience*. Cambridge, Massachusetts, London: MIT Press

Von Uexküll, J. (1992) A stroll through the worlds of animals and men: A picture book of invisible worlds. *Semiotica*, **89** (4): 319-391

Chapter 2
Avarguès-Weber, A., Mota, T. and Giurfa, M. (2012) New vistas on honey bee vision. *Apidologie*, **43** (3): 244-268

Bagnall, R., Russell, A., Brosnan, M. and Maras, K. (2022) Deceptive behaviour in autism: A scoping review. *Autism*, **26**(2): 293-307

Baron-Cohen, S. (2001) Theory of mind development in normal development and autism. *Prisme*, **34**: 174-183

Bloom, P. and German, T.P., (2000) Two reasons to abandon the false belief task as a test of theory of mind. *Cognition*, **77**(1), pp:B25-B31

Chomsky, N. (2000) *New Horizons in the Study of Language and Mind*. Cambridge: Cambridge University Press

Gaertner, L. and Schopler, J. (1998) Perceived ingroup entitativity and intergroup bias: An interconnection of self and others. *European Journal of Social Psychology*, **28** (6): 963-980

Gernsbacher, M.A. and Yergeau, M. (2019) Empirical failures of the claim that autistic people lack a theory of mind. *Archives of scientific psychology*, **7** (1): 102-118

Higgins, W.C., Kaplan, D.M., Deschrijver, E. and Ross, R.M. (2023) Construct validity evidence reporting practices for the Reading the mind in the eyes test: A systematic scoping review. *Clinical Psychology Review*, p.102378

Karban, R., Yang, L.H. and Edwards, K.F. (2014) Volatile communication between plants that affects herbivory: A meta-analysis. *Ecology Letters*, **17** (1): 44-52

Koudenburg, N., Postmes, T. and Gordijn, E.H. (2017) Beyond content of conversation: The role of conversational form in the emergence and regulation of social structure. *Personality and Social Psychology Review*, **21** (1): 50-71

Kraft, P., Evangelista, C., Dacke, M., Labhart, T. and Srinivasan, M.V. (2011) Honeybee navigation: following routes using polarized-light cues. *Philosophical Transactions of the Royal Society B: Biological Sciences*, **366** (1565): 703-708

Krupenye, C. and Call, J. (2019) Theory of mind in animals: Current and future directions. *Wiley Interdisciplinary Reviews: Cognitive Science*, **10** (6): e1503

Origgi, G. and Sperber, D. (2000) Evolution, communication, and the proper function of language. In P. Carruthers & A. Chamberlain (eds.), *Evolution and the Human Mind: Language, Modularity and Social Cognition*. Cambridge: Cambridge University Press

Peterson, C. and Wellman, H. (2019) Longitudinal Theory of Mind (ToM) Development From Preschool to Adolescence With and Without ToM Delay. *Child Development*, **90** (6): 1917-1934

Premack, D. and Woodruff, G. (1978) Does the chimpanzee have a theory of mind? *Behavioral and Brain Sciences*, **1** (4): 515-526

Riddle, S. (2016) How bees see and why it matters. *Bee Culture: The Magazine of American Bee Keeping*. Available at: https://www.beeculture.com/bees-see-matters/

Samson, D. and Apperly, I. A. (2010) There is more to mind reading than having theory of mind concepts: New directions in theory of mind research. *Infant and Child Development*, **19** (5): 443-454

Thompson, E. (2004) Life and mind: From autopoiesis to neurophenomenology. A tribute to Francisco Varela. *Phenomenology and The Cognitive Sciences*, **3** (4): 381-398

Tickle-Degnen, L. and Rosenthal, R. (1990) The nature of rapport and its nonverbal correlates. *Psychological Inquiry*, **1** (4): 285-293

Tyler, N., Stokkan, K.A., Hogg, C., Nellemann, C., Vistnes, A.I. and Jeffery, G. (2014) Ultraviolet vision and avoidance of power lines in birds and mammals. *Conservation Biology*, **28** (3): 630- 631

Chapter 3

Gigerenzer, G. and Todd, P. (1999) Fast and frugal heuristics: the adaptive toolbox. In Gigerenzer, G., Todd, P. and the ABC Research Group (eds.), *Simple Heuristics That Make Us Smart*. Oxford: Oxford University Press

Grice, P. (1975a) Logic and Conversation. In Cole, et al. (eds) *Syntax and Semantics 3: Speech Acts*: 41-58

Grice, P. (1989) *Studies in the Way of Words*. Cambridge, Massachusetts: Harvard University Press.

Sperber, D. and Wilson, D. (1986) *Relevance: Communication and Cognition*. Oxford: Blackwell Publishers

Sperber, D. and Wilson, D. (1995) *Relevance: Communication and Cognition (Second Edition)*. Oxford: Wiley-Blackwell

Van Der Henst, J.B., Carles, L. and Sperber, D. (2002) Truthfulness and relevance in telling the time. *Mind & Language*, **17** (5): 457-466

Wilson, D. and Sperber, D. (2004) Relevance Theory. In L. Horn & G. Ward (eds.), *The Handbook of Pragmatics*. Oxford: Blackwell Publishing

Chapter 4

American Psychiatric Association and American Psychiatric Association "DSM-5 task force." (2013) *Diagnostic and Statistical Manual of Mental Disorders: DSM-5*. (5th ed.) Washington, DC: American Psychiatric Association

Baron-Cohen, S., Leslie, A.M. and Frith, U. (1985) Does the autistic child have a "theory of mind"? *Cognition*, **21**(1): 37-46

Beardon, L. (2007) *Is Autism a Disorder?* (blog post) Available online at: https://blogs.shu.ac.uk/autism/?doing_wp_cron = 1544087443.5603170394897460937500#

Bleuler, E. (1911) *Dementia Praecox oder Gruppe der Schizophrenien*. Leipzig, Germany: Deuticke

Bogdashina, O. (2016) *Sensory perceptual issues in autism and Asperger's syndrome: Different sensory experiences – different perceptual worlds*. Jessica Kingsley Publishers.

Botha, M. (2020) *Autistic community connectedness as a buffer against the effects of minority stress* (Doctoral dissertation, University of Surrey).

Botha, M. and Frost, D.M. (2020) Extending the minority stress model to understand mental health problems experienced by the autistic population. *Society and Mental Health*, **10**(1):20-34

Centers for Disease Control and Prevention (CDC) (2023). *Data and Statistics on ASD*. Available online at: https://www.cdc.gov/ncbddd/autism/data.html

Chapman, R. and Carel, H. (2022) Neurodiversity, epistemic injustice, and the good human life. *Journal of Social Philosophy*, **53**(4): 614-631

Chown, N. (2016) *Understanding and evaluating autism theory*. Jessica Kingsley Publishers

Czech, H. (2018) Hans Asperger, national socialism, and "race hygiene" in Nazi-era Vienna. *Molecular autism*, **9**: 1-43

Dawson, M., Soulières, I., Gernsbacher, M. A. and Mottron, L. (2007) The level and nature of autistic intelligence. *Psychological Science*, **18** (8): 657-662

De Jaegher, H. (2013) Embodiment and sense-making in autism. *Frontiers in Integrative Neuroscience*, **7** (Article 1): 1-19

Erickson, L. (2016) Transforming Cultures of (Un) Desirability: Creating Cultures of Resistance. *Graduate Journal of Social Science*, **12** (1): 11-22

Evans, B. (2017) *The Metamorphosis of Autism*. Manchester University Press

Fein, E. (2018) Autism as a Mode of Engagement. In Fein, E. and Rios, C. (eds.), *Autism in Translation: An Intercultural Conversation on Autism Spectrum Conditions*. Switzerland: Palgrave Macmillan

Frith, U. and Happé (1994) Autism: Beyond "theory of mind". *Cognition*, **50** (1): 115-132

Graby, S. (2015) Neurodiversity: Bridging the gap between the disabled people's movement and the mental health system survivors' movement. In Spandler, H., Anderson, J. and Sapey, B. (eds.) *Madness, Distress and the Politics of Disablement*. Bristol: Policy Press

Grandin, T., & Panek, R. (2014). *The autistic brain: Exploring the strength of a different kind of mind*. Rider Books

Grant, A., Williams, G.L., Williams, K. and Woods, R. (2023) Unmet need, epistemic injustice and early death: how social policy for Autistic adults in England and Wales fails to slay Beveridge's Five Giants. *Social Policy Review 35: Analysis and Debate in Social Policy, 2023*: 239-257

Grinker, R.R. (2016) What in the world is autism? A cross-cultural perspective. In Brown, P.J. and Closser (eds.) *Understanding and applying medical anthropology* (3rd edn.). London / New York: Routledge.

Happé, F. and Frith, U. (2006) The weak coherence account: detail-focused cognitive style in autism spectrum disorders. *Journal of Autism and Developmental Disorders*, **36** (1): 5-25

Happé, F. and Frith, U. (2020) Annual Research Review: Looking back to look forward–changes in the concept of autism and implications for future research. *Journal of Child Psychology and Psychiatry*, **61** (3): 218-232

Happé, F., Booth, R., Charlton, R. and Hughes, C. (2006) Executive function deficits in autism spectrum disorders and attention-deficit/hyperactivity disorder: examining profiles across domains and ages. *Brain and Cognition*, **61** (1): 25-39

Hill, E.L. (2004) Executive dysfunction in autism. *Trends in Cognitive Sciences*, **8** (1): 26-32

Jones, D.R., Nicolaidis, C., Ellwood, L.J., Garcia, A., Johnson, K.R., Lopez, K. and Waisman, T.C. (2020) An expert discussion on structural racism in autism research and practice. *Autism in Adulthood*, **2**(4): 273-281

Leslie, A.M. and Frith, U. (1988) Autistic children's understanding of seeing, knowing and believing. *British Journal of Developmental Psychology*, **6** (4): 315-324

Kanner, L. (1943) Autistic disturbances of affective contact. *Nervous Child*, **2** (3): 217- 250

Lorde, A. (1984) *Sister Outsider: Essays and Speeches by Audre Lorde*. Reprint. New York: Crossing Press, Random House (2007)

Manning, C., Williams, G.L. and MacLennan, K. (2023) Sensory-inclusive spaces for autistic people: We need to build the evidence base. *Autism*, **27**(6): 1511-1515

Milton, D. (2012a) *So what exactly is autism? AET Competence framework for theDepartment for Education*. Available at: http://www.aettrainingehubs.org.uk/wpcontent/uploads/2012/08/1_So-what-exactly-is-autism.pdf

Morsanyi, K., Handley, S. J. and Evans, J. S. B. T. (2009) Heuristics and biases in autism: less biased but not more logical. In Taatgen, N. A. & van Rijn, H. (eds.) *Proceedings of the 31st Annual Conference of the Cognitive Science Society*

Murray, D., Lesser, M. and Lawson, W. (2005) Attention, monotropism and the diagnostic criteria for autism. *Autism*, **9** (2): 139-156

Nicolaïdis C. (2012) What can physicians learn from the neurodiversity movement? *American Medical Association Journal of Ethics*, **14** (6): 503-510

Oliver, M. (1983) *Social Work with Disabled People*. Practical Social Work Series, BASW.

Pellicano, E. (2014) A future made together: new directions in the ethics of autism research. *Journal of Research in Special Educational Needs*, **14** (3): 200-204

Proff, I., Williams, G.L., Quadt, L. and Garfinkel, S.N. (2022) Sensory processing in autism across exteroceptive and interoceptive domains. *Psychology & Neuroscience*, **15**(2): 105-130

Roberts, J. (2023) Ableism, Code-Switching, and Camouflaging: A Letter to the Editor on Gerlach-Houck and DeThorne. *Language, Speech, and Hearing Services in Schools*, 1-7 (Ahead of issue)

Robertson S. M. and Ne'eman A. D. (2008) Autistic acceptance, the college campus, and technology: Growth of neurodiversity in society and academia. *Disability Studies Quarterly*, **28** (4): np

Shah, A. and Frith, U. (1983) An islet of ability in autistic children: A research note. *Journal of child Psychology and Psychiatry*, **24** (4): 613-620

Sher, D.A. and Gibson, J.L. (2023) Pioneering, prodigious and perspicacious: Grunya Efimovna Sukhareva's life and contribution to conceptualising autism and schizophrenia. *European child & adolescent psychiatry*, **32**(3): 475-490

Silberman, S. (2017) *Neurotribes: The legacy of autism and how to think smarter about people who think differently*. Atlantic Books.

Sinclair, J. (1993) Don't mourn for us. *Our Voice* (Autism Network International newsletter), **3** (1): 1-4

Swettenham, J., Remington, A., Murphy, P., Feuerstein, M., Grim, K. and Lavie, N. (2014) Seeing the unseen: Autism involves reduced susceptibility to inattentional blindness. *Neuropsychology*, **28** (4): 563-591

The NHS Information Centre, Community and Mental Health Team, Brugha, T. *et al.* (2012) *Estimating the prevalence of autism spectrum conditions in adults: extending the 2007 Adult Psychiatric Morbidity Survey*. Leeds: NHS Information Centre for Health and Social Care. Available at: https://digital.nhs.uk/data-andinformation/publications/statistical/estimating-the-prevalence-of-autism-spectrumconditions-in-adults

Walker, N. (2021) *Neuroqueer Heresies: Notes on the Neurodiversity Paradigm, Autistic Empowerment, and Postnormal Possibilities*. Autonomous Press.

Westminster Commission on Autism (2021) Support Surrounding Diagnosis. Available from: https://www.bath.ac.uk/publications/resources-for-researchers-and-the-autism-community/attachments/support-surrounding-diagnosis.pdf

Yergeau, M. (2013) Clinically significant disturbance: On theorists who theorize theory of mind. *Disability Studies Quarterly*, **33** (4). Available online at: http://dx.doi.org/10.18061/dsq.v33i4.3876

Yergeau, M. (2017) *Authoring Autism: On Rhetoric and Neurological Queerness*. Durham, USA: Duke University Press

Chapter 5

Baggs, A. "Mel." (2007, January 15). *In My Language* [Video]. YouTube. Available online at: https://youtu.be/JnylM1hI2jc?si=72QoxL6ZDmFx3t_F

Baron-Cohen, S. (1990) Autism: A Specific Cognitive Disorder of Mind-Blindness'. *International Review of Psychiatry*, **2** (1): 81-90

Bogdashina, O. (2005) *Communication issues in autism and Asperger syndrome: Do we speak the same language?* London / Philadelphia: Jessica Kingsley Publishers

Carston, R. (1998) Informativeness, relevance and scalar implicature. In Carston, R. and Uchida, S. (eds.) *Relevance theory: Applications and implications* (Vol. 37). Amsterdam /Philadelphia: John Benjamins Publishing

Chevallier, C., Wilson, D., Happé, F. and Noveck, I. (2010) Scalar inferences in autism spectrum disorders. *Journal of Autism and Developmental Disorders*, **40** (9): 1104-1117

Cohn, E.G., Harrison, M.J. and McVilly, K.R. (2023) 'Let me tell you, I see echolalia as being a part of my son's identity': Exploring echolalia as an expression of neurodiversity from a parental perspective. *Autism*, p.13623613231195795.

Dinishak, J. and Akhtar, N. (2013) A critical examination of mindblindness as a metaphor for autism. *Child Development Perspectives*, **7** (2): 110-114

Gernsbacher, M.A., Morson, E.M. and Grace, E.J. (2016) Language and speech in autism. *Annual Review of Linguistics*, **2**: 413-425

Happé, F. G. (1991) The autobiographical writings of three Asperger syndrome adults: Problems of interpretation and implications for theory. In Frith, U. (ed.) *Autism and Asperger Syndrome*. Cambridge: CUP: 207-242

Happé, F. G. (1995) Understanding minds and metaphors: Insights from the study of figurative language in autism. *Metaphor and Symbol*, **10** (4): 275-295

Heasman, B., Williams, G. L. Charura, D., Hamilton, L., Milton, D., Vaughan, R., (forthcoming) Reconceptualising Flow States for Research on Autism. *Journal for the Theory of Social Behaviour* [in press]

Hubbard, D.J., Faso, D.J., Assmann, P.F. and Sasson, N.J. (2017) Production and perception of emotional prosody by adults with autism spectrum disorder. *Autism Research*,

Kugler, P. (2002) *The Alchemy of Discourse: Image, Sound and Psyche*. New York: Daimon

McCann, J. and Peppé, S. (2003) Prosody in autism spectrum disorders: a critical review. *International Journal of Language & Communication Disorders*, **38** (4): 325-350

Morrison, K.E., DeBrabander, K.M., Faso, D.J. and Sasson, N.J. (2019a) Variability in first impressions of autistic adults made by neurotypical raters is driven more by characteristics of the rater than by characteristics of autistic adults. *Autism*, **23** (7): 1817-1829

Naigles, L.R., Cheng, M., Rattanasone, N.X., Tek, S., Khetrapal, N., Fein, D. and Demuth, K. (2016) "You're telling me!" The prevalence and predictors of pronoun reversals in children with autism spectrum disorders and typical development. *Research in Autism Spectrum Disorders*, **27**: 11-20

Ochs, E. (2012) Experiencing language. *Anthropological Theory*, **12** (2): 142-160

Ochs, E. and Solomon, O. (2010) Autistic sociality. *Ethos*, **38** (1): 69-92

Pijnacker, J., Hagoort, P., Buitelaar, J., Teunisse, J.P. and Geurts, B. (2009) Pragmatic inferences in high-functioning adults with autism and Asperger syndrome. *Journal of Autism and Developmental Disorders*, **39** (4): 607

Prizant, B.M. (1982) Gestalt language and gestalt processing in autism. *Topics in Language Disorders*, **3**(1): 16-23

Schegloff, E.A. (1992) Repair after next turn: The last structurally provided defense (sic) of intersubjectivity in conversation. *American Journal of Sociology*, **97** (5): 1295-1345

Sirota, K.G. (2010) Narratives of distinction: Personal life narrative as a technology of the self in the everyday lives and relational worlds of children with autism. *Ethos*, **38** (1): 93-115

Solomon, O. and Bagatell, N. (2010) Introduction: Autism: Rethinking the Possibilities. *Ethos*, **38** (1): 1-7

Sterponi, L. (2018) Commentary: Words, Voice, Silence. *Autism in Translation: An Intercultural Conversation on Autism Spectrum Conditions*: 175-181

Sterponi, L. and Fasulo, A. (2010) "How to go on": intersubjectivity and progressivity in the communication of a child with autism. *Ethos*, **38** (1): 116-142

Sterponi, L. and de Kirby, K. (2016) A multidimensional reappraisal of language in autism: Insights from a discourse analytic study. *Journal of Autism and Developmental Disorders*, **46** (2): 394-405

Stribling, P., Rae, J., Dickerson, P. and Dautenhahn, K. (2006) "Spelling it Out": The Design, Delivery, and Placement of Delayed Echolalic Utterances by a Child with an Autistic Spectrum Disorder. *Issues in Applied Linguistics*, **15** (1): 3-32

Tager-Flusberg, H. (1996) Brief report: Current theory and research on language and communication in autism. *Journal of Autism and Developmental Disorders*, **26** (2): 169-172

Tager-Flusberg, H. (1999) A psychological approach to understanding the social and language impairments in autism. *International Review of Psychiatry*, **11** (4): 325-334

Walker, N. (2019) *Transformative Somatic Practices and Autistic Potentials: An Autoethnographic Exploration* (Doctoral dissertation, California Institute of Integral Studies). Available at: https://www.proquest.com/openview/e80b77f7f73b23c3cffbf0d332d94cdb/1?pq-origsite = gscholar&cbl = 18750&diss = y

Walsh, I.P., Delmar, P. and Jagoe, C. (2018) "It's Not the Asperger's That Causes the Anxiety, It's the Communication" : Person-centered Outcomes of Hope and Recovery in a Cultural–clinical Borderland. *Topics in Language Disorders*, **38** (2): 108-125

Wharton, T. (2012) Pragmatics and prosody. In Allan, K. and Jaszczolt, K.M. (eds.), *The Cambridge Handbook of Pragmatics*. Cambridge: Cambridge University Press

Wing, L. and Gould, J. (1979) Severe Impairments of Social Interaction and Associated Abnormalities in Children: Epidemiology and Classification. *Journal of Autism and Childhood Schizophrenia.*, **9**: 11-29

Chapter 6

Brewer, R., Biotti, F., Catmur, C., Press, C., Happé, F., Cook, R. and Bird, G. (2016) Can neurotypical individuals read autistic facial expressions? Atypical production of emotional facial expressions in autism spectrum disorders. *Autism Research*, **9** (2): 262-271

Cage, E. and Burton, H. (2019) Gender differences in the first impressions of autistic adults. *Autism Research*, **12** (10): 1495-1504

Cola, M.L., Plate, S., Yankowitz, L., Petrulla, V., Bateman, L., Zampella, C.J., de Marchena, A., Pandey, J., Schultz, R.T. and Parish-Morris, J. (2020). Sex differences in the first impressions made by girls and boys with autism. *Molecular Autism*, **11** (49): 1-12

Crompton, C.J., Fletcher-Watson, S. and Ropar, D. (2019a) "I never realised everybody felt as happy as I do when I am around autistic people": a thematic analysis of autistic adults' relationships with autistic and neurotypical friends and family. *Autism*, **24** (6): 1438-1448

Crompton, C.J., Fletcher-Watson, S. and Ropar, D. (2019b) Autistic peer to peer information transfer is highly effective. *Autism*, **24** (7): 1704-1712

Crompton, C.J., Ropar, D., Evans-Williams, C.V., Flynn, E.G. and Fletcher-Watson, S. (2020) Autistic peer-to-peer information transfer is highly effective. *Autism*, **24**(7): 1704-1712

Doherty, M., Neilson, S., O'Sullivan, J., Carravallah, L., Johnson, M., Cullen, W. and Shaw, S.C.K. (2022). Barriers to healthcare and self-reported adverse outcomes for autistic adults: a cross-sectional study. *BMJ Open*, **12**(2), p.e056904

Edey, R., Cook, J., Brewer, R., Johnson, M.H., Bird, G. and Press, C. (2016) Interaction takes two: Typical adults exhibit mind-blindness towards those with autism spectrum disorder. *Journal of Abnormal Psychology*, **125** (7): 879-908

Heasman, B. and Gillespie, A. (2018) Perspective-taking is two-sided: Misunderstandings between people with Asperger's syndrome and their family members. *Autism*, **22**(6): 740-750

Heasman, B. and Gillespie, A., (2019) Neurodivergent intersubjectivity: Distinctive features of how autistic people create shared understanding. *Autism*, **23**(4): 910-921

Hubbard, D.J., Faso, D.J., Assmann, P.F. and Sasson, N.J. (2017) Production and perception of emotional prosody by adults with autism spectrum disorder. *Autism Research*, **10** (12): 1991-2001

Milton, D. (2012b) On the ontological status of autism: the double empathy problem. *Disability and Society.* **27** (6): 883-887

Milton D., Heasman B. and Sheppard E. (2018) Double Empathy. In: Volkmar F. (ed.) *Encyclopedia of Autism Spectrum Disorders*. New York: Springer

Morrison, K.E., DeBrabander, K.M., Faso, D.J. and Sasson, N.J. (2019a) Variability in first impressions of autistic adults made by neurotypical raters is driven more by characteristics of the rater than by characteristics of autistic adults. *Autism*, **23** (7): 1817-1829

Morrison, K.E., DeBrabander, K.M., Jones, D.R., Faso, D.J., Ackerman, R.A. and Sasson, N.J. (2019b). Outcomes of real-world social interaction for autistic adults paired with autistic compared to typically developing partners. *Autism*, **24** (5): 1067-1080

Pearson, A. and Rose, K. (2023) *Autistic Masking: Understanding Identity Management and the Role of Stigma*. Pavilion Publishing

Quadt, L., Williams, G.L., Mulcahy, J., Larsson, D.E., Silva, M., Arnold, A.J., Critchley, H.D. and Garfinkel, S.N. (2023) "I'm Trying to Reach Out, I'm Trying to Find My People": A Mixed-Methods Investigation of the Link Between Sensory Differences, Loneliness, and Mental Health in Autistic and Nonautistic Adults. *Autism in Adulthood*. Ahead of print: DOI:10.1089/aut.2022.0062

Sasson, N.J., Faso, D.J., Nugent, J., Lovell, S., Kennedy, D.P. and Grossman, R.B. (2017) Neurotypical peers are less willing to interact with those with autism based on thin slice judgments. *Scientific Reports*, **7** (1): 40700

Sheppard, E., Pillai, D., Wong, G.T.L., Ropar, D. and Mitchell, P. (2016) How easy is it to read the minds of people with autism spectrum disorder? *Journal of Autism and Developmental Disorders*, **46** (4): 1247-1254

Williams, G. L. (2020) From anonymous subject to engaged stakeholder: Enriching participant experience in autistic-language-use research. *Research For All*, **4** (2): 314-28

Williams, G.L. Wharton, T. and Jagoe, C. (2021) Mutual (mis)understanding: reframing autistic pragmatic 'impairments' using relevance theory. *Frontiers in Psychology. Autism: Innovations and Future Directions in Psychological Research* (12): 616664. DOI: 10.3389/fpsyg.2021.616664

Zablotsky, B., Bradshaw, C.P., Anderson, C.M. and Law, P. (2014) Risk factors for bullying among children with autism spectrum disorders. *Autism*, **18** (4): 419-427

Chapter 7

Bolis, D., Balsters, J., Wenderoth, N., Becchio, C. and Schilbach, L. (2017) Beyond autism: introducing the dialectical misattunement hypothesis and a bayesian account of intersubjectivity. *Psychopathology*, **50** (6): 355-372

Botvinick, M. and Cohen, J. (1998) Rubber hands 'feel' touch that eyes see. *Nature*, **391** (6669): 756-756

Clark, A. (2015) *Surfing uncertainty: Prediction, Action, and the Embodied Mind*. Oxford University Press.

Cogo, A. (2009) Accommodating difference in ELF conversations: A study of pragmatic strategies. In Mauranen, A. and Ranta, E.(eds.), *English as a lingua franca: Studies and findings*. Cambridge: Cambridge Scholars Publishing.

Conway, J.R., Catmur, C., & Bird, G. (2019) Understanding Individual Differences in Theory of Mind via Representation of Minds, Not Mental States. *Psychonomic Bulletin and Review*, **26** (3): 798-812

Conway, J., Coll, M.P., Cuve, H.C., Koletsi, S., Bronitt, N., Catmur, C. and Bird, G. (2019) Understanding how minds vary relates to skill in inferring mental states, personality, and intelligence. *Journal of Experimental Psychology: General*, **149** (6): 1032-1047

Crystal, D. (2008) Two thousand million? *English Today*, **93**: 3-6

Cuffari, E.C., Di Paolo, E. and De Jaegher, H. (2015) From participatory sense-making to language: there and back again. *Phenomenology and the Cognitive Sciences* **14** (4): 1089-1125

De Jaegher, H. (2013) Embodiment and sense-making in autism. *Frontiers in Integrative Neuroscience*, **7** (Article 1): 1-19

De Jaegher, H. and Di Paolo, E. (2008) Making sense in participation: An enactive approach to social cognition. *Emerging Communication*, **10** (1): 33-47

Di Paolo, E.A., Cuffari, E.C. and De Jaegher, H. (2018) *Linguistic Bodies: The Continuity between Life and Language*. Massachusetts: MIT Press

Firth, A. (1996) The discursive accomplishment of normality: On 'lingua franca' English and conversation analysis. *Journal of Pragmatics*, **26** (2): 237-259

Firth, A. (2009) The lingua franca factor. *Intercultural Pragmatics*, **6** (2): 147-170

Friston K.J. (2003) Learning and inference in the brain. *Neural Network*, **16**: 1325–1352

Friston, K. J. (2016) The bayesian savant. *Biological Psychiatry*, **80** (2): 87-89

Friston, K.J., Lawson, R. and Frith, C.D. (2013) On hyperpriors and hypopriors: comment on Pellicano and Burr. *Trends in Cognitive Sciences*, **17** (1): 1

Graddol, D. (2006) *English Next* (Vol. 62). London: British Council.

Hall, C. (2018) Cognitive perspectives on English as a lingua franca. In In Jenkins, J., Baker, W., Dewey, M. (eds.). *The Routledge Handbook of English as a Lingua Franca*. London /New York: Routledge

Hillary, A. (2020a) Neurodiversity and cross-cultural communication. In: Rosqvist-Bertilsdotter, H., Chown, N. and Stenning, A. (eds.). *Neurodiversity Studies: A New Critical Paradigm*. London / New York: Routledge

Jenkins, J. (2000) *The Phonology of English as an International Language*. Oxford: OUP

Jenkins, J. (2006) Current perspectives on teaching world Englishes and English as a lingua franca. *Tesol Quarterly*, **40** (1): 157-181

Jenkins, J., Cogo, A. and Dewey, M. (2011) Review of developments in research into English as a lingua franca. *Language Teaching*, **44** (3): 281-315

Pellicano, E. and Burr, D. (2012) When the world becomes 'too real': a Bayesian explanation of autistic perception. *Trends in Cognitive Sciences*, **16** (10): 504-510

Pullin, P. (2013) Achieving "comity": The role of linguistic stance in business English as a lingua franca (BELF) meetings. *Journal of English as a Lingua Franca*, **2** (1): 1-23

Seidlhofer, B. (2011) *Understanding English as a Lingua Franca*. Oxford: Oxford University Press

Sifakis, N. and Bayyurt, Y. (2018) ELF-aware teaching, learning and teacher development. In Jenkins, J., Baker, W., Dewey, M. (eds.). *The Routledge Handbook of English as a Lingua Franca*. London / New York: Routledge

Valentine, T. (1991) A unified account of the effects of distinctiveness, inversion, and race in face recognition. *The Quarterly Journal of Experimental Psychology Section A*, **43** (2): 161-204

Vygotsky L. S. (1978) *Mind in Society: The Development of Higher Psychological Processes.* Cambridge, MA: Harvard University Press. (Original work 1930-1935)

Young, T.J. & Sachdev, I. (2011) Intercultural communicative competence: exploring English language teachers' beliefs and practices. *Language Awareness*, **20** (2): 81-98

Chapter 8

Anderson, L.K. (2023) Autistic experiences of applied behavior analysis. *Autism*, **27**(3): 737-750.

Baum, S.H., Stevenson, R.A. and Wallace, M.T. (2015) Behavioral, perceptual, and neural alterations in sensory and multisensory function in autism spectrum disorder. *Progress in neurobiology*, **134**: 140-160

Chapman, R. (2019) Autism as a Form of Life: Wittgenstein and the Psychological Coherence of Autism . *Metaphilosophy*, **50** (4): 421-440

Chown, N. (2012) *A Treatise on Language Methods and Language-Games in Autism* [Doctoral dissertation, Sheffield Hallam University]. Available at: http://shura.shu.ac.uk/7164/

Happé, F. G. (1991) The autobiographical writings of three Asperger syndrome adults: Problems of interpretation and implications for theory. In Frith, U. (ed.) *Autism and Asperger Syndrome*. Cambridge: CUP: 207-242

Happé, F. G. (1993) Communicative competence and theory of mind in autism: A test of relevance theory. *Cognition*, **48** (2): 101-119

Happé, F. G. (1995) Understanding minds and metaphors: Insights from the study of figurative language in autism. *Metaphor and Symbol*, **10** (4): 275-295

Jackson-Perry, D., Rosqvist, H.B., Annable, J.L. and Kourti, M. (2020) Sensory strangers: Travels in normate sensory worlds', in Rosqvist, H.B., Chown, N. and Stenning, A. (eds.), *Neurodiversity studies: A new critical paradigm*. Routledge

Karmiloff-Smith, A. (2006) The tortuous route from genes to behavior: A neuroconstructivist approach. *Cognitive, Affective, & Behavioral Neuroscience*, **6** (1): 9-17

Karmiloff-Smith, A. (2009) Nativism versus neuroconstructivism: rethinking the study of evelopmental disorders. *Developmental Psychology*, **45** (1): 56-63

Leinonen, E. and Kerbel, D. (1999) Relevance theory and pragmatic impairment. International *Journal of Language & Communication Disorders*, **34** (4): 367-390

Leinonen, E. and Ryder, N. (2008) Relevance Theory and Communication Disorders. In Ball, M.J., Perkins, M.R., Müller, N. and Howard, S. (eds.) *The Handbook of Clinical Linguistics*. Blackwell: Cambridge

Loukusa, S., Leinonen, E., Kuusikko, S., Jussila, K., Mattila, M.L., Ryder, N., Ebeling, H. and Moilanen, I. (2007) Use of context in pragmatic language comprehension by children with Asperger syndrome or high-functioning autism. *Journal of Autism and Developmental Disorders*, **37** (6): 1049-1059

Milton, D. (2017) *A Mismatch of Salience*. Hove: Pavilion Publishing

Nagel, T. (1974) What is it like to be a bat? *The Philosophical Review*, **83** (4): 435-450

Papp, S. (2006) A relevance-theoretic account of the development and deficits of theory of mind in normally developing children and individuals with autism. *Theory & Psychology*, **16** (2): 141-161

Wearing, C. (2010) Autism, metaphor and relevance theory. *Mind & Language*, **25** (2): 196-216

Wharton, T. (2014) What words mean is a matter of what people mean by them. *Linguagem Em (Dis) Curso*, **14** (3): 473-488

Wharton and Kolaiti (2024) *Language, Literature and Art: The Composite Organism*. Cambridge: Cambridge University Press

Chapter 9

Bargiela, S., Steward, R. and Mandy, W. (2016) The experiences of late-diagnosed women with autism spectrum conditions: An investigation of the female autism phenotype. *Journal of Autism and Developmental Disorders*, **46** (10): 3281-3294

Blood, L., Williams, G. L., Gutherson, P. & Shaw, S. C. K. (2023) Neurodiversity and Homelessness: Summary of Findings. *National Development Team for Inclusion*. Available at: https://www.ndti.org.uk/assets/files/Neurodiversity-and-Homelessness-Executive-Summary-July-2023.pdf

Blood, L., Williams, G. L., and Shaw, S. C. K. (in prep) "Society doesn't care about you": a qualitative life-mapping study of neurodivergent people's experiences of homelessness. [in preparation]

Buck, T. R., Viskochil, J., Farley, M., Coon, H., McMahon, W. M., Morgan, J., & Bilder, D. A. (2014) Psychiatric comorbidity and medication use in adults with autism spectrum disorder. *Journal of Autism and Developmental Disorders*, **44**(12), 3063-3071.

Durkheim, E. (1897) *Le suicide: étude de sociologie*. Alcan (ed.). Paris: Ancienne Librairie Germer Baillière

Haruvi-Lamdan, N., Horesh, D., Zohar, S., Kraus, M. and Golan, O. (2020) Autism Spectrum Disorder and Post-Traumatic Stress Disorder: An unexplored co-occurrence of conditions. *Autism*, **24** (4): 884-898

Hedley, D., Uljarević, M., Wilmot, M., Richdale, A. and Dissanayake, C. (2018) Understanding depression and thoughts of self-harm in autism: a potential mechanism involving loneliness. *Research in Autism Spectrum Disorders*, **46**: 1-7

Hirvikoski T, Mittendorfer-Rutz E, Boman M, Larsson H, Lichtenstein P, Bölte S. (2016) Premature mortality in autism spectrum disorder. *British Journal of Psychiatry*. Doi: 10.1192/bjp.bp.114.160192

Holt-Lunstad, J., Smith, T.B. and Layton, J.B. (2010) Social relationships and mortality risk: a meta-analytic review. *PLoS medicine*, **7** (7): e1000316

Jeste, D.V., Lee, E.E. and Cacioppo, S. (2020) Battling the Modern Behavioral Epidemic of Loneliness: Suggestions for Research and Interventions. *JAMA Psychiatry*, **77** (6): 553-554

Mason, D., Ingham, B., Urbanowicz, A., Michael, C., Birtles, H., Woodbury-Smith, M., Brown, T., James, I., Scarlett, C., Nicolaidis, C. and Parr, J.R. (2019) A systematic review of what barriers and facilitators prevent and enable physical healthcare services access for autistic adults. *Journal of Autism and Developmental Disorders*, **49**(8), pp.3387-3400

Mandy, W. (2023) The old and the new way of understanding autistic lives: Reflections on the life of Donald Triplett, the first person diagnosed as autistic. *Autism*, **27**(7), pp.1853-1855

Mayes S, Gorman A, Hillwig-Garcia J, et al. (2013) Suicide ideation and attempts in children with autism. *Research in Autism Spectrum Disorders* **7**: 109-119

MacLennan, K., Woolley, C., @21andsensory, E., Heasman, B., Starns, J., George, B. and Manning, C., (2023) "It is a big spider web of things": Sensory experiences of autistic adults in public spaces. *Autism in Adulthood*, **5**(4), pp.411-422

Mazurek, M.O. (2014) Loneliness, friendship, and well-being in adults with autism spectrum disorders. *Autism*, **18** (3): 223-232

McGraw, J.G. (1995) Loneliness, its nature and forms: An existential perspective. *Man and World*, **28** (1): 43-64

Moyse, R. (2021) Missing: The autistic girls absent from mainstream secondary schools (Doctoral dissertation, University of Reading)

National Autistic Society (2018) Hidden crisis: Autistic people four times more likely to be lonely than general public Available at: https://www.autism.org.uk/get-involved/mediacentre/news/2018-04-25-hidden-crisis-autism-and-loneliness.aspx ei

Parmar, K.R., Porter, C.S., Dickinson, C.M., Pelham, J., Baimbridge, P. and Gowen, E. (2021) Visual sensory experiences from the viewpoint of autistic adults. *Frontiers in Psychology*, **12**, p.633037

Pearson, A., Rees, J. and Forster, S. (2022) "This was just how this friendship worked": Experiences of interpersonal victimization among autistic adults. *Autism in Adulthood*, **4**(2): 141-150

Pearson, A., Rose, K. and Rees, J. (2023) 'I felt like I deserved it because I was autistic': Understanding the impact of interpersonal victimisation in the lives of autistic people. *Autism*, 27(2): 500-511

Perlman, D. and Peplau, L. (1981) Toward a social psychology of loneliness. In Duck, S. and Gilmour, R. (eds.) *Personal Relationships in Disorder*. London: Academic Press

Raymaker, D.M., McDonald, K.E., Ashkenazy, E., Gerrity, M., Baggs, A.M., Kripke, C., Hourston, S. and Nicolaidis, C. (2017) Barriers to healthcare: Instrument development and comparison between autistic adults and adults with and without other disabilities. *Autism*, 21(8): 972-984

Seeman, M. (1975) Alienation studies. *Annual Review of Sociology*, 1(1): 91-123

Stalker, K. and McArthur, K. (2012) Child abuse, child protection and disabled children: A review of recent research. *Child Abuse Review*, 21 (1): 24-40

Stauffer, J. (2015) *Ethical Loneliness: The Injustice of Not Being Heard*. New York: Columbia University Press

Sullivan, P.M. and Knutson, J.F. (2000) Maltreatment and disabilities: A population-based epidemiological study. *Child Abuse & Neglect*, 24 (10): 1257-1273

Tamás, R. (2020) *Strangers: Essays on the Human and Nonhuman*. Makina Books.

Uljarević, M., Hedley, D., Rose-Foley, K., Magiati, I., Cai, R. Y., Dissanayake, C., Richdale, A. & Trollor, J. (2020) Anxiety and Depression from Adolescence to Old Age in Autism Spectrum Disorder. *Journal of Autism and Developmental Disorders*, 50(9), 3155-3165. https://doi.org/10.1007/s10803-019-04084-z.

Valtorta, N.K., Kanaan, M., Gilbody, S., Ronzi, S. and Hanratty, B. (2016) Loneliness and social isolation as risk factors for coronary heart disease and stroke: systematic review and meta-analysis of longitudinal observational studies. *Heart*, 102 (13): 1009-1016

Weiss, J.A. and Fardella, M.A. (2018) Victimization and perpetration experiences of adults with autism. *Frontiers in Psychiatry*, 9 (Article 203): 1-10

Williams, G. L., Corbyn, J. and Hart, A. (2023) Improving the Sensory Environments of Mental Health in-patient facilities for Autistic Children and Young people. *Child Care in Practice*, 29(1): 35-53

Williams, G. L., Adams, J., Bull, P., Cave, H., Chown, N., Doherty, M., Forrest, K., Foster, R., Fricker, R., Godfree, B., Keaveney-Sheath, K., Knight, J., Marrable, T., Murray, R., Shaw, S. C. K., Ventour-Griffiths, T., Wood, J. (2022) More than words: Supporting effective communication with autistic people in health care settings. Economic and Social Research Council. Available at: https://www.england.nhs.uk/south-east/wp-content/uploads/sites/45/2022/10/More-than-words-supporting-effective-communication-with-autistic-people-in-health-care-settings-3.pdf

Wong, A., Chau, A.K., Fang, Y. and Woo, J. (2017) Illuminating the psychological experience of elderly loneliness from a societal perspective: a qualitative study of alienation between older people and society. *International Journal of Environmental Research and Public Health*, 14 (7): 824

Chapter 10

All-Party Parliamentary Group on Endometriosis (2020) *Endometriosis in the UK: time for change, APPG on Endometriosis Inquiry Report* (October, 2020). Retrieved online: www.endometriosis-uk.org/sites/default/files/files/Endometriosis%20APPG%20Report%20Oct%202020.pdf

Aspis, S. (2022) Why are disabled people with learning difficulties being prevented from leading campaigns, projects and initiatives?, *Disability & Society*, 37(1): 154-159

Autistica (2019) *Happier, Healthier, Longer Lives: Briefings to improve autism policy and research*. Available at: https://www.autistica.org.uk/downloads/files/Building-Happier-Healthier-Longer-Lives-The-Autistica-Action-Briefings-2019.pdf.

Baron-Cohen, S. (2002) The extreme male brain theory of autism. *Trends in cognitive sciences*, 6(6): 248-254

Begeer, S., El Bouk, S., Boussaid, W., Terwogt, M. M., and Koot, H. M. (2009) Underdiagnosis and referral bias of autism in ethnic minorities. *Journal of Autism and Developmental Disorders*, **39** (1): 142-148

Brown, M. and McCann, E. (2021) Homelessness and people with intellectual disabilities: A systematic review of the international research evidence. *Journal of Applied Research in Intellectual Disabilities*, **34**(2): 390-40.

Butler, J. (1990) *Gender Trouble*. London: Routledge

Cascio, M.A., Weiss, J.A. and Racine, E. (2020) Making Autism Research Inclusive by Attending to Intersectionality: a Review of the Research Ethics Literature. *Review Journal of Autism and Developmental Disorders*. DOI: 10.1007/s40489-020-00204-z

Csecs, J.L., Iodice, V., Rae, C.L., Brooke, A., Simmons, R., Quadt, L., Savage, G.K., Dowell, N.G., Prowse, F., Themelis, K. and Mathias, C.J., (2022) Joint hypermobility links neurodivergence to dysautonomia and pain. *Frontiers in psychiatry*, **12**, p.786916

Crane, L., Batty, R., Adeyinka, H., Goddard, L., Henry, L. A., & Hill, E. L. (2018). Autism diagnosis in the United Kingdom: Perspectives of autistic adults, parents and professionals. *Journal of Autism and Developmental Disorders*, **48**, 3761-3772

Crenshaw, Kimberle (1989) Demarginalizing the Intersection of Race and Sex: A Black Feminist Critique of Antidiscrimination Doctrine, Feminist Theory and Antiracist Politics, *University of Chicago Legal Forum*: **1**(8): 139-167

Crompton, C.J., Michael, C., Dawson, M. and Fletcher-Watson, S. (2020) Residential care for older autistic adults: Insights from three multiexpert summits. *Autism in Adulthood*, **2**(2): 121-127

Davidson, J. and Tamas, S. (2016) Autism and the ghost of gender. *Emotion, Space and Society*, **19**: 59-65

Department of Health and Social Care (2022) *Policy paper: Women's Health Strategy for England*. Available online at: https://www.gov.uk/government/publications/womens-health-strategy-for-england/womens-health-strategy-for-england

Durkin, M.S., Maenner, M.J., Baio, J., Christensen, D., Daniels, J., Fitzgerald, R., Imm, P., Lee, L.C., Schieve, L.A., Van Naarden Braun, K. and Wingate, M.S. (2017) Autism spectrum disorder among US children (2002–2010): Socioeconomic, racial, and ethnic disparities. *American journal of public health*, **107**(11): 1818-1826

Happé, F. and Charlton, R.A. (2012) Aging in autism spectrum disorders: A mini review. *Gerontology*, **58**(1): 70-78

Heslop, P., & Glover, G. (2015). Mortality of people with intellectual disabilities in England: A comparison of data from existing sources. *Journal of Applied Research in Intellectual Disabilities*, **28**(5), 414-422. https://doi.org/10.1111/jar.12192

George, R. and Stokes, M.A. (2018) Gender identity and sexual orientation in autism spectrum disorder. *Autism*, **22**(8): 970-982

Giwa Onaiwu, M. (2020) "They don't know, don't show, or don't care": Autism's white privilege problem. *Autism in Adulthood*, **2**(4): 270-272

Grehoua, L. (2020) Codeswitching (Radio Programme). *BBC Sounds*. Available at: https://www.bbc.co.uk/programmes/m000ls8x

Halsall, J., Clarke, C. and Crane, L. (2021) "Camouflaging" by adolescent autistic girls who attend both mainstream and specialist resource classes: Perspectives of girls, their mothers and their educators. *Autism*, **25**(7): 2074-2086

Hutson, T.M., Hassrick, E.M., Fernandes, S., Walton, J., Bouvier-Weinberg, K., Radcliffe, A. and Allen-Handy, A. (2022) "I'm just different–that's all–I'm so sorry...": Black men, ASD and the urgent need for DisCrit Theory in police encounters. *Policing: An International Journal*, **45**(3): 524-537

Hull, L., Petrides, K.V., Allison, C., Smith, P., Baron-Cohen, S., Lai, M.C. and Mandy, W. (2017) "Putting on my best normal" : social camouflaging in adults with autism spectrum conditions. *Journal of Autism and Developmental Disorders*, **47** (8): 2519-2534

Kourti, M. (2021) *Working with Autistic Transgender and Non-Binary People: Research, Practice and Experience*. Jessica Kingsley Publishers: London/ Philadelphia

Lai, M.C. and Baron-Cohen, S. (2015) Identifying the lost generation of adults with autism spectrum conditions. *The Lancet Psychiatry*, **2**(11): 1013-1027

Lai, M.C., Lin, H.Y. and Ameis, S.H. (2022) Towards equitable diagnoses for autism and attention-deficit/hyperactivity disorder across sexes and genders. *Current Opinion in Psychiatry*, **35**(2): 90-100

Limburg, J. (2021) *Letters To My Weird Sisters: On Autism and Feminism*. Atlantic Books

Liu, B.M., Paskov, K., Kent, J., McNealis, M., Sutaria, S., Dods, O., Harjadi, C., Stockham, N., Ostrovsky, A. and Wall, D.P. (2023) Racial and ethnic disparities in geographic access to autism resources across the US. *JAMA Network Open*, **6**(1), pp.e2251182-e2251182

London Assembly Health Committee (2022) *Trans health matters: improving access to healthcare for trans and gender-diverse Londoners*. Available online at: https://www.london.gov.uk/sites/default/files/health_committee_-_report_-_trans_health_matters.pdf

Lord, C., Brugha, T.S., Charman, T., Cusack, J., Dumas, G., Frazier, T., Jones, E.J., Jones, R.M., Pickles, A., State, M.W. and Taylor, J.L., (2020) Autism spectrum disorder. *Nature reviews Disease primers*, **6**(1): 1-23

Lorde, A. (1984) *Sister Outsider: Essays and Speeches by Audre Lorde*. Reprint. Crossing Press, Random House: New York (2007)

Mason, D., Stewart, G.R., Capp, S.J. and Happé, F. (2022) Older age autism research: A rapidly growing field, but still a long way to go. *Autism in Adulthood*, **4**(2): 164-172

McQuaid, G.A., Lee, N.R. and Wallace, G.L. (2022) Camouflaging in autism spectrum disorder: Examining the roles of sex, gender identity, and diagnostic timing. *Autism*, **26**(2): 552-559

Michael, C. (2016) Why we need research about autism and ageing. *Autism*, **20** (5): 515- 516

Mitchell, D. (2017) David Mitchell: almost everything I'd been told about my son's autism was wrong. *The New Statesman*. 8 July 2017 (Updated 09 Sep 2021, 5:44pm). Available online at: https://www.newstatesman.com/culture/2017/07/david-mitchell-almost-everything-i-d-been-told-about-my-son-s-autism-was-wrong

NHS Digital (2023) *Health and Care of People with Learning Disabilities, Experimental Statistics 2022 to 2023*. Available online at: https://digital.nhs.uk/data-and-information/publications/statistical/health-and-care-of-people-with-learning-disabilities/experimental-statistics-2022-to-2023

NHS England and NHS Improvement (2019) *People with a learning disability, autism or both Liaison and Diversion Managers and Practitioner resources*. Available online at: https://www.england.nhs.uk/wp-content/uploads/2020/01/Learning-disability-and-autism.pdf

Oakley, A. (1972/1985) *Sex, Gender and Society*. London: Temple Smith.

Gov.UK (2023) *Ethnicity Facts and Figures*. Available online at: https://www.ethnicity-facts-figures.service.gov.uk/health/mental-health/detentions-under-the-mental-health-act/latest/

Office for National Statistics (2023) ONS website, statistical bulletin, *Gender identity, England and Wales: Census 2021*. (Released 6 January 2023)

Perez, C.C. (2019) *Invisible women: Data bias in a world designed for men*. Abrams.

Phillip, R. (2022) Overpoliced and adultified: how the justice system is failing autistic Black people. *gal-dem* [website article]. Published 14 September 2022. Available online at: https://gal-dem.com/overpoliced-adultified-police-failing-black-autistic-people/

Rose, V., Trembath, D., Keen, D. and Paynter, J. (2016) The proportion of minimally verbal children with autism spectrum disorder in a community-based early intervention programme. *Journal of Intellectual Disability Research*, **60**(5): 464-477

Savarese, D. J. (2021) December 25). Disrupting the garden walls. *Logic Magazine*. (25 December 2021). Available online at: https://logicmag.io/beacons/dismantling-thegarden/

Santinele Martino, A. and Fudge Schormans, A. (2018) When good intentions backfire: University research ethics review and the intimate lives of people labeled with intellectual disabilities. In *Forum Qualitative Sozialforschung/Forum: Qualitative Social Research* (Vol. 19, No. 3, p. 18). DEU.

Seers, K. and Hogg, R. (2023) "Fake it 'till you make it": Authenticity and wellbeing in late diagnosed autistic women. *Feminism & Psychology*, **33**(1): 23-41

Social Care Institute for Excellence (2017) *Improving Access to Social Care for Adults with Autism*. Available at: https://www.scie.org.uk/autism/adults

Social Care, Local Government and Care Partnership Directorate (2014) *Think Autism. Fulfilling and Rewarding Lives, the strategy for adults with autism in England: an update*. Available online at: https://assets.publishing.service.gov.uk/government/uploads/system/uploads/attachment_data/file/299866/Autism_Strategy.pdf

Solanke, I. (2022) The anti-stigma principle and legal protection from fattism. In *Legislating Fatness* (pp. 49-67). Routledge.

Steinbrenner, Jessica R., Nancy McIntyre, Lindsay F. Rentschler, Jamie N. Pearson, Paul Luelmo, Maria Elizabeth Jaramillo, Brian A. Boyd et al. (2022) "Patterns in reporting and participant inclusion related to race and ethnicity in autism intervention literature: Data from a large-scale systematic review of evidence-based practices." *Autism* **26**, no. 8 (2022): 2026-2040

Tilley, E., Christian, P., Ledger, S. and Walmsley, J. (2021) Madhouse: Reclaiming the history of learning difficulties through acting and activism. *Journal of Literary & Cultural Disability Studies*, **15**(3), pp.347-363

Wake, W., Endlich, E., Lagos, R. (2021) *Older Autistic Adults: In their own words*. Kansas, USA: AAPC Publishing

Walker, A. (2018) Why the UK needs a social policy on ageing. *Journal of Social Policy*, **47** (2): 253-273

Warrier, V., Greenberg, D.M., Weir, E., Buckingham, C., Smith, P., Lai, M.C., Allison, C. and Baron-Cohen, S. (2020) Elevated rates of autism, other neurodevelopmental and psychiatric diagnoses, and autistic traits in transgender and gender-diverse individuals. *Nature communications*, **11**(1): 3959

West E. A., Travers J. C., Kemper T. D., Liberty L. M., Cote D. L., McCollow M. M., Stansberry Brusnahan L. L. (2016). Racial and ethnic diversity of participants in research supporting evidence-based practices for learners with autism spectrum disorder. *The Journal of Special Education*, **50**(3), 151-163

Westergaard, D., Moseley, P., Karuna Hemmingsen Sørup, F., Baldi, P., Brunak, S. (2019) Population-wide analysis of differences in disease progression patterns in men and women. *Nature Communications*,**10** (1)

Westminster Commission on Autism (2021) *Support Surrounding Diagnosis: An Inquiry into Pre- and Post- Support for the Autism Diagnosis Pathway*. Available online at: https://www.bath.ac.uk/publications/resources-for-researchers-and-the-autism-community/attachments/support-surrounding-diagnosis.pdf

Wilkinson, L.A. (2008) The Gender Gap in Asperger Syndrome: Where are the Girls? *TEACHING Exceptional Children Plus*, **4**(4) Article 3

Williams, G. L., Ellis, R., Axbey, H., Grant, A. (2024) *Autistic, hysteric: Inequity in the United Kingdom's healthcare for Autistic people with wombs*. In Milton, D. (ed.) *The Double Empathy Problem Reader*. Hove: Pavilion Publishing

Williams, R.M. (2020) Falsified incompetence and other lies the positivists told me. *Canadian Journal of Disability Studies*, **9**(5): 214-244

Wu, J., Gale, C.P., Hall, M., Dondo, T.B., Metcalfe, E., Oliver, G., Batin, P.D., Hemingway, H., Timmis, A. and West, R.M. (2018) Editor's Choice-Impact of initial hospital diagnosis on mortality for acute myocardial infarction: A national cohort study. *European Heart Journal: Acute Cardiovascular Care*, **7**(2): 139-148

Wyatt, T.A. and Seymour, H.N. (1988) The Implications of Code-Switching in Black English Speakers. *Integrated Education*, **24** (4): 17-18

Young, V.A. (2009) " Nah, We Straight": An Argument Against Code Switching. *JAC* (29): 49-76

Chapter 11

Anzaldúa, G. (1987) *Borderlands/ La Frontera: The New Mestiza* (4th ed.). San Francisco: Aunt Lute

Bhabha, H. (1994). *The Location of Culture*. London: Routledge

Ikas, K. and Wagner, G. (eds.) (2009) *Communicating in the Third Space*. Routledge: New York/Oxon